THE
COMPLETE
WOMAN
GOLFER

THE
COMPLETE

WOMAN GOLFER

Vivien Saunders

Stanley Paul

London Melbourne Sydney Auckland Johannesburg

FOREWORD

It has always been rather a mystery to me, and very sad, that more women have not produced sporting books of an instructional nature. Many outstanding sportswomen clearly have so much invaluable knowledge to pass down to future generations. I was therefore delighted when I heard that Vivien Saunders had written an instructional book for the many hundreds of thousands of women playing golf in the British Isles today.

The Complete Woman Golfer is beautifully illustrated by that ace photographer, Peter Dazeley, and is packed full of good sound common sense.

Over the years golf instructional books have tended to become increasingly technical and some are so complicated that the reader is forced to assume either that the author is a genius or that he himself is of below average intelligence. The truth of course is that these books are almost impossible to understand for anyone but a professional with an academic approach to the game.

I am delighted to say that Vivien Saunders' book does not fall into this category. It is straightforward, clear instruction on a level that any golf enthusiast can digest and put into practice. Incidentally it will be of enormous help to any male golfer who gets hold of a copy. There are, however, many special lessons that are specifically for women golfers and it is for this market that Vivien Saunders writes.

This is a much needed book, and one which I am extremely pleased to recommend.

Peter Alliss

ACKNOWLEDGEMENTS

Although this is a golf book by a woman and for women golfers, there are a number of men to whom credit must go for its production. Firstly, there are five very fine golf professionals to whom my thanks must go – Bill Cox, Syd Scott, Eddie Ward, Howard White and John Jacobs. The five of them have been almost entirely responsible for teaching me everything I know about the golf swing and instilling in me the art of teaching the game to others. Without them there is no doubt whatsoever that I – and, indeed, many other prominent players of my age – would not be in the positions they are today.

Secondly, I am indebted to the secretaries and members of the Tyrrells Wood, Leatherhead and Worplesdon Golf Clubs for kindly letting me use their courses for taking the pictures which figure in this book. I have also received valuable technical assistance from Mr. John Ovenstone and the other directors of Nicoll of Scotland and from Mr. Dick Penfold of Golf Ball Developments.

Lastly, my thanks go to Peter Dazeley who spent many days patiently taking and processing the pictures which play such an important part in this book and to Lewis Pollock for the drawing and artwork on these which I hope brings out the most essential points in the instruction.

Stanley Paul & Co. Ltd, 62-65 Chandos Place, London WC2N 4NW. An imprint of Century Hutchinson Ltd.
London Melbourne Auckland Johannesburg and agencies throughout the world.
First published 1975, reprinted 1977, 1980, 1982, 1984, 1986.
© Vivien Saunders 1975. Photographs © Peter Dazeley 1975.
Set in VIP Helvetica. Printed and bound in Great Britain by Anchor Brendon Ltd, Tiptree, Essex.
ISBN 0 09 124090 5

CONTENTS

1 THE GRIP

Why the grip is so important

One of the main difficulties in writing an instructional golf book is to persuade the established golfer to read slowly and patiently through the pages and chapters on the real basics of the game.

Golf is unlike many other games or skills where what one learns as a raw beginner becomes so automatic and simple that it never need be reviewed again. Take driving a car for example. After the first few lessons one never finds oneself forgetting which pedal is which or which way to turn the wheel because they are simple movements which become second nature. In golf, however, the initial lessons on grip and stance never lose their importance and, in fact, often become all the more vital the better and better player one becomes. The fault of many established players is that they don't realize just how much there is to be learnt about both grip and stance so that they don't go hunting for further knowledge. This is a great mis-

take. Good golf is thoroughly dependent on good basics, but they are basics which need to be reviewed periodically and adapted as the overall swing moulds itself in one way or another.

The grip, which is, after all, one's only physical contact with the club, is just as subtle as it seems simple. It plays a vital part in each factor of striking the ball. It controls the power and distance one achieves. It determines the type of height one is likely to produce. And it dictates whether one hooks or slices – in other words, whether the ball bends to the left or right in the air. For the good player it isn't just a question of having one set grip and sticking to it through thick and thin. No, the grip can be made to work for you in producing the full range of shots necessary for top class golf. If, that is, you fully understand it. So, before you decide to turn to the pages beyond the basics, take a long and rather critical look at your own grip to see

whether your knowledge of it is as full and thorough as it might be.

Let's get one thing clear, however. There is no definite right and wrong way of gripping the club. The grip will need to vary from one person to another; the grip which is just right for me isn't necessarily the one which is just right for you. One needs to learn how the grip controls the shots one produces in order to find the grip most suitable to one's own swing. You will probably even find that as your swing develops and improves so your grip may need adjusting along with it. It isn't something one can learn as a beginner and then assume to be perfect for evermore.

Try to learn not only the basics of the grip but also the importance of the minor adjustments one can make to it. Then, at the first sign of any trouble in the game, return to this as the most fundamental principle in the golf swing.

Stage by stage through the grip

The first stage in the grip should be to sole the club on the ground so that the face is perfectly square. In other words it is aimed directly on target with the line along the *bottom* of the clubhead – not the top – facing squarely down the fairway. A good grip without this preliminary aiming of the clubface is quite meaningless. One of the chief purposes of the grip, and in fact the whole swing, is to return

the clubface squarely to the ball. So start with it there, steadying it with the right hand.

The left hand
To form the grip, let the left hand hang loosely down by the side of the club, with the fingers relaxed so that they hang vertically. This brings the club across the palm of the hand in a diagonal way, from the first joint of the index

finger towards the heel of the hand (Fig. 1). This diagonal relationship is most important. From this, as the hand is folded over, the thumb and first joint of the index finger appear to be very nearly level with one another (Fig. 2). This we call the 'short thumb'.

The mistake of the beginner, particularly amongst women, is for so much effort to be put into getting the left hand firmly on

1

2

3

the club that the diagonal relationship is immediately lost (Fig. 3). The left hand is now straight around the shaft instead of diagonally on it and as the grip is completed the thumb slips far down the club (Fig. 4). This not only gives looseness throughout the swing but makes the right hand very difficult to position on the club, the left thumb poking through the thumb and index finger of the right.

So, position the club diagonally against the left hand by soling it squarely on the ground and hanging the fingers loosely against it, the thumb appearing short and pulled well up on the grip.

Checkpoints

The player's view of this sees the line or 'V' in between the thumb and index finger pointing up somewhere between the chin and right shoulder; for the beginner the most suitable position for this 'V' being right to the shoulder (Fig. 5). Notice too just how close the thumb and index finger are, so that the two are in contact very nearly to the end of the thumb. If they ever stray far apart, correct positioning of the right hand is made virtually impossible.

As a further checkpoint, one can get a very good idea of the suitability of the grip from the number of knuckles showing. The player should see the first and second knuckles quite clearly, plus all or part of the third knuckle, but never the whole of the fourth. Again the grip is likely to vary slightly with the standard of the player, the beginner using a 'three knuckle grip', in which, as the name implies, the first three knuckles all show, while the experienced, low handicap golfer may well do better with a 'two knuckle grip'.

Adding the right hand

To form the simplest type of grip – the 'baseball grip' – rest the club on the middle joints of the fingers of the right hand, so that

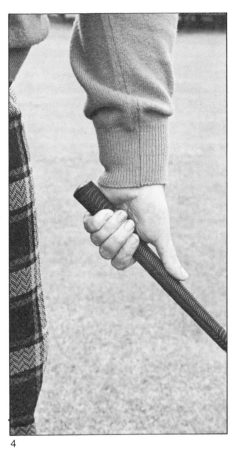

4

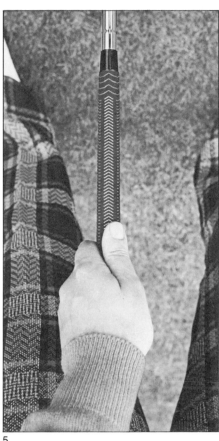

5

1. The left hand hangs loosely against the side of the club so that it crosses the palm diagonally from the first joint of the index finger to the heel of the hand.

2. In the correct left hand grip the top of the thumb and first joint of the index finger are approximately level – the short thumb.

3. Incorrect. The hand is straining to get round the grip, the club lying straight across the fingers.

4. Incorrect. Without the diagonal positioning the thumb stretches too far down the shaft.

5. The 'V' between thumb and index finger points up between the chin and right shoulder, the thumb and index finger being kept close together.

all eight fingers are on the club with no gaps between them. As you begin to fold the right hand over onto the club, feel the palm of the right hand facing down the fairway to your target, so that it is very much *behind* the club. Now try to fit the left thumb snugly into the fleshy pocket in the palm of the right hand. The base of the left thumb should now rest very comfortably into the fold at the bottom of the right palm (Fig. 6).

With the right hand completely folded over the club, the left thumb should be almost entirely covered, with the relationship between the thumb and index finger of the right hand fol-lowing very much the pattern of the left. Once more the tip of the thumb and first joint of the index finger are just about level with one another. Here again, let's stress the importance of the closeness of the left thumb and index finger. Correct positioning of the right hand centres almost entirely on the position of the left thumb, and if the left thumb is allowed to stray away to the right of the shaft, the right hand is forced under instead of behind the club.

Looking at your own grip

The player's view of the completed grip also shows both hands following the same type of pattern; the line or 'V' in between the thumb and index finger again pointing somewhere between the chin and right shoulder, and ideally absolutely parallel with that of the left (Fig. 7). The long handicap woman golfer and beginner will usually do best with both these lines pointing directly to the right shoulder; the professional, by contrast, will often have a grip to match a more powerful swing where the lines point right to the chin. Basically, however, if one keeps these lines or 'V's parallel with one another and pointing somewhere between the right shoulder and chin, no major fault is likely to arise in the grip.

6. The club is rested on the middle joints of the fingers of the right hand with the fold in the right hand being brought against the base of the left thumb.

7. The 'V' in between the thumb and index finger of the right hand is parallel with that of the left, again pointing between the chin and right shoulder.

8. The Vardon grip. The right little finger is hooked round the outside of the index finger of the left hand, keeping the hands working close together.

9. The interlocking grip. The little finger of the right hand and index finger of the left are hooked together, being ideal for the golfer with short fingers.

6

7

Welding the hands in the grip

One of the simplest ways of learning to grip the club for the beginner is the baseball grip which I have just described, in which all eight fingers are on the club. The hands can then be set very much to the sides of the club and all the important fundamentals of the grip adopted. However, the ordinary baseball grip does have one severe drawback; this is that the hands easily tend to slip apart so that instead of working in harmony they tend to work in oppo-

8

9

sition to one another. More ideally, then, we work on a type of grip which provides some type of linkage between the hands. There are two main ways of doing this, in each case linking the adjoining fingers of the hands – the little finger of the right and the index finger of the left.

The Vardon grip

The first of these and more widely taught, I suppose, is the 'Vardon grip' – named after the great British professional, Harry Vardon, who popularized it. In this, the right little finger is hooked around the outside of the first joint of the index finger of the left so that only seven fingers are now in contact with the club; the hands, however, are securely joined (Fig. 8). This is an excellent grip for those who can do it. Unfortunately it is not suitable for all golfers, particularly women. Firstly, a woman's hands are often different from a man's in that the little finger of a woman's is often considerably shorter, making this overlap very awkward. Secondly, many

players who take up golf in later life and who don't work with their hands have distinct difficulty in separating the first three fingers of the right hand from the little one. This means that as they try to achieve this overlap the middle finger also creeps up on top of the other hand and the control necessary in the right one is lost.

To form the Vardon grip, the little finger of the right hand must be most definitely separated from the other three. The club is then rested on the middle joints of these three fingers, pulling them up close to the left hand, while the little finger is hooked around the outside of the left hand index finger. If you can get this separation of the little finger from the others quite simply, then the Vardon grip is probably the one for you.

The Nicklaus or interlocking grip

For anyone starting golf in or beyond middle age, or for the golfer with small hands or rather short fingers, there is another alternative. This is the inter-

locking grip – the one used by Jack Nicklaus. In this case the adjoining fingers are linked by hooking them together, both finger tips outwards, so that the length of the little finger of the right is relatively unimportant (Fig. 9). This provides excellent cohesion between the two and also means that if the left hand is positioned correctly the right can hardly help but follow. As a rule I start the beginner with the Vardon grip, not because of any technical advantage, but rather because it is more widely used. But if the player shows any sign of awkwardness in learning the grip I immediately adopt the interlocking grip which generally seems to be that little bit easier to learn and repeat correctly.

So these are the three main grips in golf – the Vardon grip, the interlocking grip and the baseball grip. Between the first two there is little to choose except personal ease and comfort, but the baseball grip I would always rate a very poor third because it fails to unite the hands and lets them work in opposition to one another.

How tightly should I grip?

This is such a common question from beginners, and yet it is awfully hard to answer in a concrete way. Many men professionals will say that they hold the club extremely lightly, yet I often wonder whether a man's idea of holding lightly and a woman's idea of holding firmly don't amount to roughly the same thing. The error amongst most women golfers is that the grip is too loose so that the club

turns in the hands on impact with the ball. I certainly don't hold the club as tightly as I could or my knuckles would begin to show white and my wrists would become rigid and locked. But I hold firmly, perhaps at 90 per cent strength. For the natural games player this is fairly instinctive; one holds the golf club with the same type of pressure one grips a tennis racquet. You don't want to let it go, and

yet you don't want to create excessive tension. What is important is that one sets the firmness of the grip and maintains it right through the swing; it should never tighten as the swing starts or the whole character of the grip can often change quite crucially. So setting the pressure in the grip is just as important a part of the preparation as setting the hands themselves.

10 and 11. Incorrect. The right hand is beneath and not behind the club, the 'V's pointing well outside the right shoulder. At impact the right hand comes through palm to the target, turning the clubface into this closed position, producing shots which fly low and to the left.

10

11

Limits of the Grip

Golf is a game in which the spin put on the ball is most important. Just as the ball takes up back-spin, which keeps it flying through the air, so it takes up sidespin which makes it curve in flight; for a right-handed player a hook curving to the left and a slice to the right. It is the exact positioning of the hands on the club which is very largely responsible for the spin put on the ball.

Basically, in a sound grip, the hands are very much to the sides of the club with the palm of the right hand facing powerfully down the fairway to the target. In fact, this position, in which the right hand is directed to the target, is so instinctive to the human body that however the right hand is positioned at address it will manoeuvre itself into this position as the ball is struck. What is *not* instinctive is to set the right hand in this way at address. The instinctive way to grip a club is to position the

right hand very much under the shaft. This feels great. Not only does it feel strong because it supports the weight of the club, but it also gives the impression of being able to scoop the ball upwards into the air. But, and this is the crushing fault of this grip, as the arms swing down to the ball the right hand comes in with the palm to the target. In doing so it twists the clubface back into a 'closed' or left-aimed position (Figs. 10 and 11). This has the effect of both tending to send the ball curving away to the

left and, often more noticeable to the woman golfer, reducing quite drastically the height and carry of the shots. True, this grip does feel most natural and comfortable until one can grasp the idea of setting the power of the right hand to the target and not under the shaft.

If by contrast the right hand starts very much on top of the club at address, it will twist the club into an 'open', or right-aimed, position at impact (Figs. 12 and 13). This causes the ball to curve away to the right, often

12

13

12 and 13. Incorrect. The right hand is very much on top of the club, the 'V's pointing left of the chin. At impact the right hand comes through behind the club, turning the face into an open position, producing shots which fly high and to the right.

with rather exaggerated height.

Grip adjustment and direction

So the more we turn the right, or right and left hands, to the right on the club, the more likely we are to hook the ball – and the less likely we are to slice it. The more we turn the hands to the left on the club, the more likely we are to slice the ball – and the less likely we are to hook it. This therefore gives us the key to most hook and slice problems and a relatively easy way of be-

ginning to control either problem.

A slice can be stopped by moving the hands to the right on the club and a hook cured by moving both hands to the left. But, there are most definite limits to this grip outside which one is likely to meet other problems. The 'V's between the thumb and index fingers of both hands are the key to this, for at all times the 'V's should stay quite easily visible to the player, and pointing up between the chin and right shoulder. The nearer you move

the 'V's to the right shoulder the more you discourage a slice, and the nearer you move them to the chin the more you discourage a hook. However, the chin and right shoulder should be looked upon as the absolute limits of all adjustments.

Summing up

This, then, is the grip. It isn't difficult; in fact it is very easy. What is difficult is to realize just how important it can be to every class of golfer. Many a scratch golfer and professional has struggled away to cure a fault which he assumed to be in the swing, when all the time the answer lay in the fundamentals of the grip. Perhaps as few as 5 per cent of club golfers grip the club correctly and as few as 1 per cent really understand the intricacies of the grip. Most golfers, however, cannot accept that any serious fault can lie in such a simple part of the swing. It almost seems to be a matter of pride that one shuns the idea of dealing with such basics at any sign of trouble. So don't be a proud golfer; be a realistic golfer and periodically take a critical look at your grip to see whether it really is just as good as you probably assume.

2 THE ADDRESS POSITION

The basic set-up

The address position serves several purposes; it shouldn't just be a question of standing in a rather haphazard way to the ball and expecting to hit it on target just through swinging in the right way. The set-up plays a very large part in enabling the player to get the very best from her swing. It should aim both the clubface and swing in the right direction, prepare the muscles for the correct actions throughout the swing itself, and then help in starting everything into action for the shot.

As a beginner, the address position will probably seem very simple and unimportant, but as one becomes a better and better player, hitting the ball longer distances, the way in which one stands comes to play a very large part in the success of the shot. Indeed one usually finds with the experienced golfer that most changes in the swing which lead to loss of form start with some fault in the set-up. On the other hand, faults which creep into the address position are often much more easily rectified than if one tries to make a change to the swing itself. So it pays to spend plenty of time learning to set-up well to the ball.

Although the address position needs to be looked at thoroughly, the last thing one wants is to force the body into any type of twisted, contrived, tense position. This is unnecessary. In fact the emphasis should be on comfort and relaxation, but comfort and relaxation in the right type of position!

The feet and legs

Let's look at the very basic

14. At address the clubface is square, left arm straight, right relaxed, feet roughly hip width, knees knocked inwards but with the toes turned outwards and the weight on the insides of the feet.

address position with one of the medium irons, the 5, 6 or 7 (Fig. 14). The first step is to set the clubhead squarely behind the ball, so that it looks straight down the fairway, gripping so that the palm of the right hand too seems to be aimed on target from behind the club. In doing this, stand with the feet together directly opposite the ball, then spread each 6 inches or so to the side, so that the ball is opposite

the middle of the stance, the feet feeling a comfortable distance apart. The usual guide is to stand with the feet roughly shoulder width. However, a woman's physique usually differs from a man's in that the hips for a woman are wider than her shoulders, where for a man it is the other way round. A woman's idea of a shoulder width stance is often narrow in relation to her hips. It is the hips, after all, from where the leg action stems, so I would rather describe the width of the stance in terms of hip width than shoulder width. This should then help to throw the weight slightly onto the insides of the feet as it should be, with the knees knocked inwards and comfortably relaxed and flexed. The toes should be turned out a little, the left perhaps slightly more than the right, but without the feeling that the position is awkward.

The arms

Now for the arms. With the shaft pointing straight up towards you, let the arms hang fairly loosely downwards, so that the arms and clubshaft form a 'Y' shape. Because the right hand is below the left on the club you should find that the right shoulder has dropped a little below the left, but again don't strive to contort yourself into this position; if you don't think about it it will probably happen quite naturally. The set-up is also very much concerned with preparing the body for its movements in the swing itself, and making it as easy as possible to get into the right position through impact. As far as the arms are concerned the right arm has to fold away into the body in the backswing, while the left remains extended – a relative rôle they play right through impact. This is encouraged right from the set-up. The left hangs loosely but extended, while the right is relaxed and slightly bent into the side. To encourage the arms to fold into the side correctly – the right on the backswing and the left on the throughswing – the elbows should be pointing diagonally downwards so that the insides of the arms are clearly visible to you, not turned in to face one another. However, if this doesn't happen fairly easily don't force yourself into this position at the expense of comfort and confidence. The grip should now be firmly in control of the club, but without creating tension in the arms and wrists.

Lastly, the eyes are set very definitely on the *back* of the ball – the part you are going to hit – *not* the top of it, with the head tilted very slightly to the right, so as to be fractionally behind the ball.

Posture in the set-up

When we begin to look at the posture of the body at address, we come to a problem like the one of 'How hard do I grip the club?' The correct posture one should adopt is hard to define; it not only varies from player to player quite dramatically but it also changes for one player throughout the set of clubs. This second factor is brought about by the difference in lengths of shafts between the clubs and the angle at which they sit. This is really no great difficulty, for if one just takes up every club without trying for any specific change in posture from one to the other, the change will be made quite subconsciously. What it does mean, however, is that one cannot define posture too rigidly in terms of angles and positions. If you don't think about it you will naturally adopt a far more erect body position with the long shafted woods, and a more crouched one with the short shaft of the wedges.

Basically there are two factors to look at in the posture of the golfer. Firstly, how much does one bend over in the body, and secondly, where does one bend from? Let's take the second problem first.

Where does the body bend?

The usual fault of the inexperienced golfer and unnatural athlete is to bend in the waist and back. In setting up to the ball, the legs remain straight while the upper body is tipped forward with what only amounts to a slouching of the shoulders. This is far from correct. Now the legs are rendered lifeless and all possible power stems from the shoulders.

Correctly the bending should come from below the waist – in fact, from the top of the legs. To produce this position put your hands on your hips and have the feeling of bending yourself from the top of the legs, countering the tilting forward of the body by sticking out your bottom very slightly and also by flexing the knees. This then is an active position, rather like the one assumed in receiving service at tennis.

Now, how much should the body bend? The angle of the back varies enormously amongst tournament professionals, so that it is very difficult to say exactly what is right. All that one can really do is to examine the two extremes and the types of faults they produce, making sure that one keeps within these limits. The player who stands very erect produces, as a rule, a swing in which the shoulders turn virtually horizontally, producing a very flat swing around the body and distinct difficulty in getting good height to the shots. By contrast, the player who bends and crouches too much in the set-up produces a very vertical turn of the shoulders and high, upright swing with a tendency to dig into the ground behind the ball and to produce excessive height to the shots. I am always tempted to say that the vast majority of women beginners do not bend enough to the ball, but one then comes across the pupil at the other extreme who clearly crouches over too much, making any type of generalization somewhat dangerous. What I would say, however, is that not bending enough is more likely to cause real difficulties to the beginner than bending too much. My own posture, I would say, is fairly standard, being neither particularly crouched nor upright, so that learning from copying this (Fig. 15), bearing in mind that I am using a 6-iron, is probably rather easier than trying to define it any further.

16

17

15. Correct posture shows a bending from the top of the legs, the bottom sticking out slightly. The lines across the toes, knees, hips and shoulders are all parallel to the line of the shot, aimed at the flag in the distance.

16. The open stance. The lines of the body and clubface diverge or 'open' to the target, tending to send the ball slicing away to the right.

17. The closed stance. The line of the body and clubface converge or 'close' to the target, tending to send the ball hooking away to the left.

Direction at address

As we look at the set-up from the right of the player, in other words directly down the line of the shot, we can see the other important factor in the address position – aiming the swing at the target (Fig. 15). Hitting the ball from A to B is, after all, the chief aim of every shot and setting up to the ball is just like aiming a gun. One can't pull the trigger and hope to be on target if everything is directed wrongly to start with.

So as well as aiming the clubface at the flag we have to make it as easy as possible for the swing to travel in the right direction. The most standard way of directing the swing correctly is to position the whole body so that it is parallel to the line on which you hope to hit the ball – the 'square' stance. This is really just like standing on a pair of railway lines, with the ball to travel down the right-hand one, but the line of your feet set down the other.

The whole action, however, involves a swinging of the arms, so that it is the line of the shoulders, even more than the feet, which really controls the direction of the swing. The shoulders as a rule do not naturally fall into the correct position without some thought and adjustment. Because the right hand is below the left on the grip, this tends to pull the right shoulder forward. Add to this the fact that one is concentrating on the target and it is easy to see why the shoulders tend to be turned slightly towards the target. To get the correct square position with not just the feet, but also the knees, hips and shoulders parallel to the line of the shot, one has to have the feeling of looking at the flag very much *over* the left shoulder and not past it. This, as a rule, is almost always the most unnatural part of the address position and the part which is the greatest source of trouble to the golfer of all standards.

The open and closed stances

One very important point about the basic square stance is that it sets the direction of the swing and clubface in the same line. This is important in making the ball fly straight. Golf differs from most other ball games in that the ball all too readily takes up spin, making it curve away to the left or right – the hook and slice. This happens whenever one meets up with the ball with the swing travelling in a different direction from the clubface, in other words, when the line of the swing and clubface are at odds with one another. In the first chapter I showed how the grip controls the way in which the clubface returns to the ball, and whether the clubface is aligned with the direction of the swing through impact. But misdirecting the clubface and swing at address can bring about much the same results.

Supposing the clubface looks off to the right of target or the feet and shoulders look off to the left – or a combination of both – the lines of the body and clubface are no longer parallel but instead diverge or 'open' to the target. This we call, therefore, the 'open stance'. It tends to misdirect the line of the swing and clubface through impact and put a slice spin onto the ball which sends it curving away to the right (Fig. 16).

By contrast, if the clubface looks to the left and the feet and shoulders to the right, or a combination of both, the lines of the body and clubface converge or 'close' to the target. Hence this is known as the 'closed stance'. Once again it tends to misdirect the line of the swing and clubface through impact, this time putting a hook spin on the ball so that it bends from right to left in the air (Fig. 17).

Distance from the ball

Generally a woman golfer has to stand a little further from the ball than a man. She has, after all, a bosom to negotiate in the backswing – a problem which, of course, affects some more than others! So to keep the left arm straight throughout the backswing she often has to stretch a little to the ball. But, and here is the problem, as one reaches more and more for the ball, direction is likely to become more erratic.

Think of it this way. The clubhead travels on a somewhat circular path on the downswing, ideally approaching a straight line in the impact zone. The further one stands from the ball the more pronounced this curve becomes so that there is very little of it which approximates to a straight line through impact (Fig. 18). It is all too easy to catch the ball before or after the straight-through part of the swing is reached – often producing shots which start to right and left almost at random.

Now look what happens as one moves closer to the ball; the curve on which the clubhead travels becomes gentler and gentler (Fig. 19). It approximates far more easily to a straight line for a longer distance at the bottom of the swing. Now there is very much more chance of starting the ball on target. So in theory the closer one stands to the ball the straighter one is likely to hit it.

A very good guide to the most suitable type of distance one should stand from the ball, comes from the position of the right elbow. This should be just clear of the body (Fig. 15), perhaps a matter of an inch or so, and never, unless one's build really makes this necessary, pulled well away from the waist.

So remember this: the tendency of almost all golfers is to creep further and further from the ball, especially when confidence is high during a patch of playing well. So guard against this and be prepared to move an inch or two closer to the ball than may really feel comfortable. It will almost certainly pay dividends with added accuracy and consistency.

A pattern in the set-up

It is not only important that one learns to set-up well to the ball, but also that one learns how to repeat this position time after time. The way of doing this is to develop a very definite pattern in the way you approach every shot. This is very marked in the tournament golfer, who repeats every move from the moment he gets to the ball until he strikes it so religiously that every last hitching up of the trousers or adjustment of the glove becomes quite a trademark of the player.

True, much of this is habit and really only superfluous ritual, but what is important is that in building up such an exact pattern of actions, the tournament golfer is able to stand within a fraction of an inch of the same position every time he sets up to the ball.

The club golfer on the other hand shuffles up to the shot, placing the clubs sometimes on the right, sometimes on the left, approaching the shot in a completely haphazard way. Even this very preliminary stage is important. Get used to approaching the ball from the same side, viewing the shot from directly behind it to get a really clear picture of what you are trying to produce. Having chosen the club and had a practice swing, create a most definite pattern.

Creating a routine

The first stage is to aim the clubface at the target. This isn't quite as easy as one might assume, for the vast majority of right-handed golfers seem to aim to the right of target – largely, one assumes, because one is looking slightly sideways at it and the view is distorted. It is rather safer, I feel, not just to look at the target, but in viewing the shot from behind to pick out a spot 18 inches or so in front of the ball on line with the target, and to concentrate on lining up over this. With the clubface aimed in this way, the grip is set, feet together. Place the feet apart – first the right and then the left. (Or vice versa, the main point is repetition.) Settle yourself, check your aim and then FIRE.

Make it a really definite rou-

INCORRECT

18

tine and you will soon find that you can assume the same position over and over again, both quickly and easily. This build up to the shot soon becomes second nature. Indeed, if you watch the tournament professional, you will often see that if the concentration is broken the whole procedure is started all over again. The practice swing, the re-adjustment of the glove or hitching up of the trousers – they are all repeated. Unnecessary, you may say, but it is all part of a routine, and a routine in this way can only help in building a consistent address position and swing.

18. Incorrect. In standing too far from the ball the clubhead travels in a sharp curve around impact, tending to produce inconsistent direction.

19. As one stands closer to the ball the clubhead travels on what approximates to a straight line for much longer around impact, making it easier to strike the ball on target.

19

3 THE BACKSWING

In tackling the backswing I am going to deal with it in two very different ways. Firstly, I am going to analyse it stage by stage so that one sees exactly how the club gets from address to its position at the top of the swing. Secondly, and quite distinct from this, I am going to run through the process of how I teach the backswing. I think the distinction is very important.

Sequence pictures can be of great value in learning the swing, but only if one uses them to get a good overall picture of the action. The five pictures in the sequence of my backswing by no means represent five definite disjointed stages in my swing, or five definite thoughts in my mind. There could just as easily, space permitting, have been seven pictures, or nine pictures or fifteen pictures making up this sequence. They are there to give an overall impression of the swing. To make full use of them don't isolate each picture as a position; rather pick out the action of the arms throughout the series of pictures, then the legs, then the clubhead and try to get an impression of the continuous movement involved.

A picture of the backswing

Right from the set-up the position of the body is set to encourage the right type of action in the backswing and in turn the correct position at impact. The arms are already in the relationship they should hold through impact, with the left extended and the right relaxed and folded into the side, while the position of the legs is definitely indicative of action rather than being static and lifeless. The direction of the body, too, plays its part, with the whole body from the feet to the shoulders – and here let's stress again the importance of the shoulder line – absolutely parallel to the proposed direction of the shot, so that the shoulders return most readily to this square position at impact, encouraging correct direction to the delivery on the ball (Fig. 20).

From the address position the backswing is initiated very much as a whole, with the entire body setting the swing in action, a forward press in the right knee in my own case giving the cue for everything else to start in harmony. This naturally produces a little movement in the hands, a little movement in the arms, a little in the legs and so on, rather than any definite lead from one part of the body or the other. The very start of the takeaway, then, is smooth, with a gradual build up of speed, with the clubhead quite naturally moving low to the ground and taking up the natural arc which brings it gradually inside the line of the shot (Fig. 21).

As the backswing continues the body is kept travelling very much in unison; the shoulders continue to turn, for the woman golfer almost always necessitating a corresponding, though rather smaller, turning of the hips, while the legs give the freedom for this movement, with the left knee pointing smoothly in behind the ball but the right still flexed and concentrated very definitely on the inside of the foot. The right arm continues to fold into the body, while the left moves across the chest, still straight, so that it comes closer and closer to the right shoulder. It is this action of coming across the body which enables it to stay straight. Correct action all the way to this stage sees the back of the left hand quite naturally following the plane of the arms, never turned under to face the ground nor rolled over to look upwards (Fig. 22).

As the top of the backswing is approached the same relative actions of legs, arms and body are continued – the knees maintaining their flexed positions, weight still on the insides of the feet, with the left heel just beginning, perhaps, to feel a slight pull upwards. With the shoulders approaching a full turn, the hips continue to pivot to make this movement possible, while the left arm is now quite clearly well across the body so that it can be fully extended with the right continuing to fold into the side. Although the hands have been active in taking the club back in a co-ordinated sequence with the rest of the body, it is only comparatively late that the action of the hands reveals itself in their natural hinging or cocking movement, but there is no definite time at which one should attempt to set the hands to work in this way. They work their own way into the backswing when the need arises (Fig. 23).

As the top of the backswing is

20

21

22

reached the movements which were initiated right from the takeaway have continued to completion, so that the back is fully turned to the target, the left arm perfectly straight and across the chest so that it is tight towards the right shoulder with minimal separation between the elbows. This results in the club pointing directly down the line of the shot with, from a sound grip, the face of the club taking up very much the same angle as the left arm and in turn the whole plane of the swing. Despite the half turn of the hips, the right leg from the knee down has remained motionless, with the weight still concentrated on the inside of the foot, and the knee flexed for powerful but fluid legwork through impact (Fig. 24).

Learning the backswing

Having seen what is involved in the backswing, let's start from the beginning in actually learning the action. Vital to this next stage are a good grip, with the hands very much to the sides of the club, and a good address position in which the right arm is relaxed, with the feet hip-width apart and the weight concentrated on the insides of the feet, particularly of the right.

The 'toe-up' position

The first movement to learn is just of taking the club back to around hip-height. This is made up of two co-ordinated actions, firstly turning the shoulders and secondly bending the left knee in, heel lifting fractionally, so that it seems to point roughly towards the ball. The weight of the right foot, however, is most definitely kept on the inside of the foot so that hardly any action is noticed in the right leg. What is most important at this point, and perhaps the largest hurdle for the woman beginner, is to allow the arms to turn as the shoulders turn so that the toe of the club points directly upwards as it reaches hip-height. From a good grip the thumbs will now be virtually on top of the shaft (Fig. 25).

This 'toe-up' position is a most

23

24

essential stage for the beginner and I would suggest repeating the action time and again, watching to check that the toe of the club comes into this position quite naturally, before going any further with the swing. Let me stress that this 'toe-up' position is an essential to *learning* the swing; it is not necessarily seen in the swing of the low handicap and tournament golfer.

Finishing the backswing

The reason why this stage is so important in developing the backswing is that during the remainder of it the wrists hinge upwards as the arms travel higher. Once the club is in this 'toe-up' position, with the thumbs uppermost, they can hinge very freely, in just the same manner as they might if the club were held out in front of you

at arm's length. The backswing then becomes a continuation of the shoulder turn with the arms swinging upwards and the wrists hinging in this way. At the top of the swing the club is supported by the left thumb with the back of the left wrist slightly concave or 'cupped'.

The left knee points in still further behind the ball, the heel pulling a couple of inches off the ground, while the weight of the right foot is still concentrated on the inside of it, the right leg maintaining virtually the same flexed position it held at address (Fig. 26). Learning the backswing is then very much a two-piece action, taking the club to hip-height with the toe upwards, and from there hinging the wrists as the arms swing up higher. To start with practise it as a definite ONE, TWO action, from there gradually smoothing

it out into one movement, checking that the wrists are correctly cupped at the top of the backswing, left thumb in a supporting rôle. Let me clarify one point here. The 'cupping' of the left wrist outgrows its usefulness as a player approaches professional standard, so you will often see tournament golfers and strong men with a far straighter back to the left hand than I am advocating in developing your backswing.

The reason why I place so much emphasis on the 'toe-up' position and cupping of the left wrist is this. Generally the beginner takes the club back with the face of the club looking almost downwards as it approaches hip-height. The back of the right hand is now on top of the club, thumbs to the side (Fig. 27). From here the wrists cannot hinge correctly

25

26

27

28

but the right simply buckles and the left collapses over it as the swing reaches the top (Fig. 28).

This is clearly a weak, powerless position, but unless one stresses most strongly getting that 'toe-up' position, it is the one which most women beginners naturally fall into.

Perfecting the arm action

In describing how I teach the backswing I have purposely left out any mention of the 'straight left arm'. This is not because it is unimportant, but because I often feel that striving for this in the very first lesson inhibits the idea of swinging the club. But having learnt to take the club to the top of the backswing, with the wrists hinging correctly, I think it is now time to concentrate on the exact positioning of the arms.

The straight left arm

The straight left arm, like most things in golf, is not an absolutely hard and fast rule; a number of fine players have shown quite a bend in the elbow. But I think it makes life easier if one does learn to keep it straight. Not only does it give a

more easily repeatable position than falling into any number of bent ones, but it also adds power by creating a wider swing and prepares the left arm for being straight through impact. So, let's give it a try.

As the beginner starts to swing the club, one of two things usually happens. Either both arms bend at the elbow, or, in some cases, both arms stay wooden and stiff. What we want is for the right arm to fold neatly into the body while the left is perfectly straight. The real secret of this is for the left arm to work very much across the body towards the right shoulder. The closer the left arm can be drawn to the chest and right shoulder the easier it is to keep straight (Fig. 29). The right arm in turn can fold in neatly so that the elbow points downwards.

This action of bringing the arm across the chest is understandably a little more difficult for the amply endowed golfer to grasp than for a man or young girl! What so easily happens is that the left arm is forced out away from the body as the backswing starts. The distance between the left elbow and right shoulder is now far greater and the left arm can hardly help but bend as the backswing continues (Fig. 30). For the woman golfer who does have this problem of almost getting in the way of herself, the arms may well have to be held further from the body at address so that the left arm can be above the bosom and still tight across to the right shoulder at the top of the backswing.

Creating the right plane of swing

The other point which concerns us in dealing with the arm action

25 and 26. From the address position the first stage for the beginner is to achieve this 'toe-up' position at hip height. From here the wrists can naturally hinge as the arms swing on up, the club now supported by the thumbs at the top of the backswing.

27 and 28. Incorrect. The arms have not turned to bring the toe of the club upwards. The left hand is now below the club and not to the side of it, so that the wrists cannot hinge upwards but simply collapse in the backswing.

is that of creating a good, sound plane to the swing. This really refers to the angle on which the whole swing revolves. In the flat swing the club is taken very much around the body, where in the upright swing it is lifted high above the head. As well as depending to a great extent on the posture of the body, dealt with in the chapter on the address position, this is also very dependent on the way in which the arms fold into the

body. Again one cannot say exactly what is right or wrong, for tournament professionals vary enormously in the arm position they adopt. What one can do, however, is to show the extremes of the action which might be considered the limits of a good swing. Outside these one is likely to meet with trouble; if one can fall into a position directly between the two then this is really where the truly orthodox swing should lie.

The right elbow your key

The plane of the arms is really determined by the degree of freedom one gives to the right arm. If the elbow is kept very close to the side of the body in the backswing, the arm forms a very acute angle – less than a right angle – producing a narrow, flat swing. The shaft of the club is likely to be outside the arm and elbow when viewed from behind and also well below the top of the head (Fig. 31).

On the other hand if the right elbow is allowed to travel much further from the side of the body, it reaches the top of the swing with the arm at very much more than a right angle. The arms are no longer in a compact unit, the right elbow may be seen to fly out behind the player and the clubshaft is well above the head (Fig. 32).

To create a perfectly copybook plane, the right arm should be allowed to move just sufficiently far from the body to enable it to be approximately a right angle as the club reaches horizontal. The clubshaft will now be over the shoulder or upper arm and roughly level with the top of the head. Experiment with the freedom you give the right arm in the backswing, producing a plane which gets the best from, and avoids the worst of, either extreme (Fig. 33).

Leg action and body turn

In Figure 33 we see another real essential of the backswing – aiming the club down the line of the shot. Ideally at the top of the backswing the shoulders should be fully turned so that the club is approximately horizontal and directly on this line. This really aims the whole swing for the delivery into the ball. If the shoulder turn is insufficient the club looks to the left of the line of

29. The left arm is drawn very much across the body towards the right shoulder, elbows close together, which enables it to stay straight.

30. Incorrect. The left arm has worked out too far from the body and right shoulder, producing too much spread between the elbows and forcing the left arm to bend.

31. The right elbow has been kept very tight against the body in the backswing, producing a flat plane to the swing.

29

30

31

the shot and the downswing in turn becomes left-aimed or, to use the more common technical phrase, 'out-to-in'. The opposite, an overturn of the shoulders, can happen but this is far more unusual and more the fault of the better player. The underturn, however, happens all too easily for the average golfer and leads, as we will see later, to the most common of golfing faults, the slice.

Getting a good, full turn of the shoulders really stems right from the legs. Only with a really tall man can the shoulders be turned fully without much movement in the legs and hips. For the shorter and older woman golfer, shoulder turn, hip turn and leg action must be very strongly connected.

Hip turn and the right leg

One must, however, take great care over how the hips turn. What must *not* happen is for the hips to swivel back to such a degree that the right leg straightens or locks (Fig. 34). This renders the legs virtually powerless in the downswing and tends to throw power into the shoulders, which is far from correct. The way to produce correct action in the right leg is to concentrate the weight on the inside of the right foot at address, keeping it there throughout the backswing. This makes it almost impossible for the knee to straighten back into the locked position. If one refers back to Figure 33 and also to the sequence of my backswing (Figs. 20–24) it is clear that the

hips have now turned sufficiently but without very much actual movement in the right leg. It is still flexed and ready for action in the downswing. One further point here is that for a woman golfer in particular the left heel must be free to pull its way off the ground as the body turn takes place. This enables the right degree of hip turn to take place to produce the full shoulder turn. A tall man and even a tall or very supple woman can often create a shoulder turn without much movement in the legs, but even here it is a bad thing to try to anchor the left heel on the ground. Don't consciously lift it, but certainly give the heel freedom to move a couple of inches off the ground to give your shoulders the freedom to turn fully.

32. The right elbow has been given too much freedom to move away from the body, creating a very upright plane to the swing.

33. In a copybook plane the right elbow moves to a right angle in the backswing, the shaft of the club roughly level with the top of the head.

34. Incorrect. The right leg has swivelled back and locked making it impossible for the legs to work smoothly in the throughswing.

32

33

34

4 DOWN AND THROUGH THE BALL

Looking at the throughswing

In dealing with the through-swing I am going to tackle it in just the same way as I did the backswing – firstly discussing a sequence of shots and then dealing with how one actually learns this part of the swing. Once more benefit can be gained from the sequence by studying a part of the body right through all the pictures, giving an overall idea of the movements of, let's say, the left arm or the legs rather than trying to see the swing through as seven somewhat disjointed positions.

Let's remind ourselves of the important features of the backswing position (Fig. 35). The shoulders are fully turned so that the club points along the line of the shot, the left arm is straight with the right neatly folded to about a right angle, the left heel has been allowed to pull fractionally off the ground but the right leg has stayed virtually motionless with the knee still flexed.

Starting down

The start of the downswing is initiated with a firm pushing down of the left heel – another reason I like to see the woman golfer allowing it to rise in the backswing. It gives a definite way of changing directions in the swing. As the left heel is thrust back to the ground, the arms change directions with a definite pulling down of the left arm. This should all happen at speed so that the degree of wristcock in this initial stage of the downswing is just as it was at the top of the backswing (Fig. 36).

With the left foot firmly planted on the ground the left side of the body begins to become firm and stretched while the right side starts to shorten or compress. The left arm is perfectly straight, travelling at maximum possible speed, while the right arm is still slightly folded into the side. In other words the arms begin their work from the top of the swing as a unit so that they are in the same relative positions – the left extended and the right bent. By this stage the right knee is beginning to move its way into the shot so that both knees seem to be sliding towards the target. The body is beginning to unwind from its fully coiled position but remains predominantly behind the ball. It is as though the legs are most definitely working forwards while the body almost works back behind the ball (Fig. 37).

Impact

As impact is reached, the left arm is still travelling at maximum speed, perfectly straight, while the right arm has almost straightened, the wrists having uncocked quite naturally at this stage so that the clubhead is level with, but never ahead of, the hands. This, of course, all happens at such speed that one can hardly have any concept of the exact positioning at impact. What one can feel, however, is the position of the head – still well behind the ball – with the right side compressed, body beginning to arch, but with the legs working their way most definitely towards the target (Fig. 38).

As the action continues through impact, the proof of a good swing can usually be seen. If the left arm has been worked as fast and freely as it should have, it will still be virtually straight, with the right at last straightening fully after impact. The eyes are glued to the spot where the ball was, head held back, with the legs flexed and the left heel firmly on the ground right through this action. The body begins to come through to face the target, but without moving ahead of the ball, so that the back correctly starts to arch (Fig. 39).

Halfway through the follow-through all these actions have continued, the right knee through towards the target, the head held back, body arched and almost fully facing the target. The arms now start to reverse the rôles they played in the backswing. Just as the right then folded neatly into the body, elbow pointing down, so the left arm must be allowed to turn, elbow down, and fold into the body on the throughswing. It is a mistake to try to keep the left arm too rigid, for the wrist simply collapses or the elbow breaks outwards as the right struggles to keep up with it. With the left arm correctly turned, elbow down, the back of the right hand now faces outwards, toe of the club pointing almost directly upwards, so that the wrists can begin to hinge in just the same way as they did in the backswing (Fig. 40).

The finish

As the followthrough is completed, the left heel is firmly on the ground, not with the weight, however, all on the left foot by any means, but with it balanced between the left foot and the toes of the right. The head is still behind the spot where the ball was, back arched, so that the weight is still fairly central in the feet. Although the right arm has been straight through some of the followthrough, it is allowed to bend quite freely as the swing is completed, so that both arms are relaxed, with the wrists fully cocked once again and the club straight back over the left shoulder. At the finish, the grip should be firm and the whole body turned through to face the target, the eyes at last looking up to follow the flight of the ball (Fig. 41).

Learning the throughswing

Having dealt with an overall picture of the down and throughswing, let's look at the types of ideas one should work at in learning this stage of the swing. I think one of the simplest ways is to separate the swing into its two chief components – a turn of the body, combined with a swing of the arms.

Body and leg action

Let's start with the body and leg action. At the top of the backswing the back is fully turned to the target, the hips turned half this, the legs are flexed, with the left knee pointing in behind the ball and the heel fractionally off the ground (Fig. 35). From here the whole action is one of turning through to face the target. The left heel is pushed back to the ground, the leg rapidly

35

36

39

40

37

38

41

35–41. A picture of the throughswing.

straightening, pulling the body on through and in turn bringing the right knee round towards the target so that the foot is balanced on the toes. The whole body is now turned to the left (Figs. 36–41). So if we look at the body action through the whole swing, it is really just a turn to the right in the backswing and a turn to the left in the throughswing, giving plenty of freedom to the legs and feet.

Arm action

To this let's add the arm action. At the top of the backswing the shoulders are fully turned, the hips turned roughly half this and the arms are lifted. From here, all the arms basically do is to swing down and up to a very similar position on the other side of the body. The whole down and throughswing is essentially one of speed so that it must be developed as a continuous, fluid action *not* as a number of positions. The one position I would isolate *en route,* however, corresponds to the hip-height position in the backswing. Here I stressed how important it is in learning the backswing for the thumbs to be uppermost at this stage, toe of the club pointing directly upwards, so that the wrists can hinge naturally (Fig. 25). Just the same is true of the throughswing. We therefore have a very important position beyond impact. The arms are given the freedom to turn slightly so that once more the thumbs are on top of the club, the toe pointing directly upwards. We also have a corresponding type of leg action to the one shown in the mirror position on the backswing. The hips are

43

44

42. In starting the downswing push the left heel back to the ground and at the same time feel a pull down with the left hand and arm.

43 and 44. In learning the throughswing, the essential is to mirror the 'toe-up' position of the backswing, Fig. 25, thumbs on top. From this position the wrists can hinge upwards, both arms being allowed to bend to bring the club back over the left shoulder.

42

now turning towards the target with the right knee pointing inwards and the right heel off the ground. Only from this type of 'toe-up' position can the wrists hinge freely into a correct followthrough. Let me clarify this; this 'toe-up' position, as in the backswing, is an essential to *learning* a sound throughswing and also for the club golfer. It isn't necessarily seen in the tournament professional. The answer is really that one must *feel* this position, but in speeding up the swing it tends to be modified.

Three key points

To learn the down and throughswing let's work on a definite three-part action. Firstly assume the top of the backswing position, left heel pulled an inch or so off the ground, legs flexed and the arms in position. The first stage is to develop the right idea of the start of the downswing. To do this, push the left heel back to the ground and at the same time pull down a couple of inches with the left hand. Now let the left heel lift again and the arms rise and repeat this with an almost bouncing action. Heel down, left hand down. The movement only needs to be a matter of inches to alert the parts of the body which are responsible for changing directions (Fig. 42).

The second stage, having alerted the left heel and left hand, is to continue these movements fluently through to the hip-height position beyond the ball. The left leg straightens, right knee coming through, heel well off the ground, while both arms point out towards the target, toe of the club and thumbs uppermost (Fig. 43).

The third movement is to hinge the wrists upwards, this time letting both arms relax and bend so that the club comes straight back over the left shoulder with the thumbs largely supporting it (Fig. 44). The whole body is now turned to face the target with the right knee almost beside the left and the right foot brought through onto the toes.

Having worked on these three essentials of the throughswing it is gradually moulded into a one-piece, fluent movement, with the clubhead brushing the ground each time at the bottom of the swing.

5 PUTTING THE SWING TOGETHER

A question of timing

For the good golfer the backswing and downswing merge together so well that it is very difficult to pinpoint the end of the backswing and beginning of the throughswing. The arms may still appear to be travelling away from the ball while the lower body and legs have clearly changed directions. But for the beginner and average club golfer the swing is seen as very much a two-piece action – up and down.

Very often, however, it is the point of transition from one to the other which is the prime source of trouble. The backswing can be executed correctly and the downswing, in practice at least, can follow on. Put the two together at speed and the sudden change of directions can throw everything out of step.

Looking for power

What so easily happens is that, whereas with the practice swing there is no temptation to seek power, in the swing itself one begins to apply much more strength. This strength tends to be imparted with the shoulders and right arm. At the top of the backswing they are clearly in a strong, powerful position and it takes a very good golfer indeed to resist throwing in force from this part of the body in setting the swing in reverse. The shoulders, however, should do absolutely nothing in delivering power to the ball. Indeed the perfect swing shows the right shoulder moving very little from the top of the backswing, while the left arm swings fast and

45. In the throughswing the right shoulder travels a very small distance compared with the arms so that it is the movement of the arms which must be stressed.

freely away from it. The movement that is seen in the right shoulder is correctly the result of its having been pulled through by the speed of the left arm and drive of the legs, and *not* from a direct pushing of the shoulders themselves.

Great care must always, therefore, be taken in putting the two halves of the swing together. In the throughswing the shoulders, although eventually turning through to the target, travel a comparatively short distance with that of the hands and arms (Fig. 45). It is all too easy to

achieve this full turn through of the body and shoulders while leaving the arms lagging behind. So of our two components in the throughswing – the turn through of the body and the swinging of the arms – it is the turn through of the body which is by far the more natural. One therefore sees the club golfer in a position at impact where the body turn is far ahead of the swing of the arms (Fig. 46). This is the classic case of mis-timing and results in the most common of golfing faults – the slice.

The rules for timing

So, in putting the swing together and speeding up the action, keep these two rules clearly in mind. Firstly, power must never be generated with the shoulders. Start the downswing by pushing the left heel down to the ground to reverse the action of the legs and simultaneously swing the left arm *away* from the right shoulder.

Secondly, the arms and hands have to travel considerably further in the throughswing than do the shoulders and upper body. The whole essence of how well you put the swing together is timing the two so that they reach the followthrough position together. The shoulders must never push the arms on through, but rather the speed of the arm swing should eventually pull the shoulders through. Once they have turned fully in the backswing, the work of the shoulders is over and from there on they should assume a perfectly passive rôle.

46

47

48

46. Incorrect. The shoulders have forced power into the shot, leaving the arms and club lagging behind and producing a slice position.

47. The angle of the clubface means that by purely brushing the ground on which the ball sits the clubhead strikes the ball below centre and lofts it into the air.

48. Incorrect. In trying to lift the ball the clubhead passes up towards the top of the ball, striking it above centre and sending it rolling along the ground.

Getting under the golf ball!

After the last piece of advice which was for the golfer of all standards – even serving as a reminder to the tournament class golfer – this section is entirely devoted to the needs of the real beginner and long handicap player. Indeed, although this phrase 'getting under the golf ball' has probably struck horror into the hearts of every good golfer, it is the piece of advice which the beginner has really been waiting for.

'How, in fact, do you get under the ball? How do you lift it into the air?'

For, if there is one phrase more common from the beginner than 'I didn't keep my head down' it is this horrendous 'I didn't get under the ball.'

So, for the beginner and long handicap golfer, this is the basic piece of advice for actually hitting the ball into the air. In tennis you can get under the ball; it is struck in mid-air. To loft the ball higher and higher if you wish, you simply hit it more and more upwards. You attack it from beneath and drive it upwards into the air. Now let's look at golf. Except on the tee the ball sits on the ground, with a cushion of grass perhaps a quarter of an inch deep below it. Now the big question is this. With the ball sitting on the ground in this way, how can you get underneath it? So it certainly isn't like a tennis ball which is struck in mid-air. In fact it isn't even like a soccer ball which is both large and relatively light so that striking it below its equator gets it airborne. No, the golf ball gives us an entirely different problem.

To get a golf ball airborne one is purely dependent on using the loft of the club. Each clubface is angled back so that, providing the bottom of the clubhead comes through level with the bottom of the ball, in other words brushing the grass on which it sits, it strikes the ball below its equator and naturally lofts it into the air (Fig. 47). As the loft of the club increases, so the clubface meets the ball lower and lower below its centre. It therefore lofts it higher and higher into the air. All *you* are required to do is brush the ground on which the ball sits and the loft of the club will do the work for you.

Let me repeat, with the ball sitting on the ground, you cannot get under it. Let's see what happens if one tries to get under it and lift the ball into the air. What now happens is that the bottom of the swing falls somewhere behind the ball and as you try to lift it the clubhead actually travels upwards and, far from catching the ball on its underneath, actually comes up and hits it more towards the top. Now instead of the loft of the club working for you all that happens is that the edge of the clubhead

strikes the ball and sends it rolling along the ground (Fig. 48). The greater your efforts at getting under the ball the more this will happen.

Your first stage in learning to strike the ball is to position it on some fairly lush grass, giving a cushion between the ball and ground of perhaps half an inch, and from there, using one of the medium irons, to concentrate on

brushing away the little piece of grass on which the ball sits. Try to be patient in this, having plenty of practice swings, and then purely concentrating on brushing away the little piece of grass on which the ball sits. If you can do this the ball will rise quite simply, just taking up the natural loft of the club.

Give it a swish

Now you have reached the stage where you can put the swing together sufficiently well to get the ball airborne from this grassy type of lie, just brushing the grass on which it sits and letting the loft of the club send the ball into the air. From here we want to build up length. Hitting the ball a long way is usually fairly natural for a man; in fact most men try to hit the ball too hard. For women, however, the major handicap even into the single figure handicap range is just not being able to hit the ball far enough. It is true that amongst world class players the very longest hitters tend to be big and powerful, but to become a long hitter, certainly by club standards, muscle and strength are not required. It is far more a question of achieving the right knack – almost a throwing action or flick of the wrists.

For the professional golfer this flick of the wrists is so natural, just as in throwing a ball, that he or she is unconscious of it. In fact because the professional is more concerned with accuracy as a rule than with distance, the natural flick of the wrists almost has to be curbed.

But not so with the average woman golfer and beginner. With these players the hands and wrists need most definite training. To develop this knack of a flick of the wrists one needs a strange combination of firmness and looseness in the muscles; one wants firm, perfect control with the hands and yet looseness in the wrists and arms to permit them to travel at speed. Try this experiment. Without holding a club, stiffen up your left arm and swing it in front of you. Now relax it and feel the difference as it swings. The first feels strong, but it is with the second that all the speed can be felt. So the first hurdle is to develop this idea of relaxation and speed, not force.

The wrist action

Now let's look at the wrist action which gives the good golfer the swish of the clubhead through the ball. From the top of the backswing the arms start down as a unit so that the left stays straight, the right bent and, most important in this context, the wrists still cocked. This is just the result of a rapid change of

directions and pull in the left arm (Fig. 49). By the time the arms reach this type of height in the throughswing, however, the wrists have turned and cocked in the other direction (Fig. 50). Although, therefore, the hands have only travelled a distance of 3 or 4 feet, the clubhead has travelled through an arc of something like 15 feet, meaning that the clubhead is travelling something like four times as fast as you can make your hands travel.

Training the wrists and hands

Perhaps the best way of training the hands to develop this clubhead speed is to practise swinging with the feet together. This immediately puts emphasis on the hands and arms, for the body and legs are virtually immobilized. The feeling must definitely be one of throwing the clubhead through the ball, letting the wrists be perfectly loose and relaxed. As one practises this the arms should be allowed to turn quite freely, the right folding into the body on the backswing and the left into the body on the throughswing. The thumbs are now correctly

49 and 50. In the correct action the hands whip the clubhead through so that the clubhead travels very much further than the hands. This generates speed through impact. For women this 'throwing' action usually needs definite training.

49

50

uppermost as the hands reach hip-height both back and through, giving the wrists the freedom to hinge correctly, not folding back on themselves. Swing the club back and through, back and through repeatedly and really get those wrists loose and free, throwing the clubhead through the ball.

I am one of the last people to advocate loose, wristy play for the top class woman golfer. She, after all, has reached or almost reached her full potential for length. But the club golfer, as a rule, needs all the distance she can produce; this has to be developed by training the hands and wrists and creating that all-important 'swish' as the ball is struck.

Hit <u>through</u> the ball, not <u>to</u> the ball

Having developed the idea of achieving length through a knack of flicking the wrists, the other essential of long-hitting is to concentrate on hitting right through the ball. What so easily happens is that one looks at the ball and only 'thinks' of hitting at it. What in fact happens is that the mind subconsciously resists this impact and actually starts slowing up before the clubhead ever gets to the ball. One may feel one is hitting the ball awfully hard, but part of the energy expended is actually used to put on the brakes. The follow-through of the swing then becomes short and unsteady and the ball just doesn't fly as far as one might expect.

I think the best analogy to draw is of a karate chop. Having placed a piece of wood across two solid objects to form a kind of bridge, the karate expert would tell me that I could drive my hand right down through the wood. In myself, however, I feel inhibited. However hard I try to hit it my mind tells my body to resist the impact and all I can do is give the wood a rather unconvincing thump, hurting myself much more than I damage the wood! The expert apparently tackles this quite differently. His sights are set, not on the plank as mine were, but on the floor beneath. He raises his hand and drives it right on through towards the floor, accelerating through the plank and smashing it in two.

This is the kind of idea one needs in the golf swing. The idea is to hit the ball, but the whole aim must be of hitting right through to the finish. It is the followthrough and not the ball which becomes the mental aim of speed in the downswing. For this reason you will almost always see the professional, except perhaps in punching a short iron, swinging right on through to a really long finish. The tremendous speed generated quite naturally takes the swing on to this length. The club golfer, by contrast, very rarely displays much followthrough at all. If you swing right *through* the ball and not *to* the ball the followthrough should take the club well on over your left shoulder and past the horizontal.

The importance of the finish

So, although what one does after the ball is struck cannot actually affect the flight of the ball, the followthrough is just as important a part of the action as is the backswing. It serves two very vital purposes. Firstly, it gives something to aim at, both in speed and position. If one can accelerate from a sound position at the top of the backswing to an equally good position in the followthrough, the intermediate action through the ball is certain to be fairly acceptable. Secondly, it gives one a checkpoint for much of what has gone before in the swing. There are three important points one can check in the finish of the swing – firstly, that the grip is just the same and just as firm as it was at address; secondly, that although one has turned to follow the flight of the ball the head is in much the same position as it started, weight balanced between the left foot and toes of the right, back slightly arched; and thirdly, that the body is facing down the fairway to the target.

So, remember, the swing does not end at the ball. Try to accelerate right through beyond the ball to a really good, firm finish, holding it for a definite count of two or three. Thinking of the follow through really does help create maximum speed through impact and holding the finish gives you a checkpoint for everything that has gone before.

6 USING THE FULL SET OF CLUBS

Most of your work as a beginner will have been done with the medium irons, the 5, 6 and 7. These are logical clubs to begin with, partly because they come in the middle of the range of clubs, and partly because they are often the simplest. Now one gets to the point of playing round the course and needing to use the rest of the clubs to produce a variety of lengths of full shots. Although the clubs are quite different in character and in the length of flight they produce, the swing itself stays basically the same throughout. The swing you learnt for the medium irons stands you in good stead for hitting everything else from wedge to driver.

The short irons

Let's look first at the short irons – our accuracy clubs. These, the 8, 9, 10 (or pitching wedge) and sand wedge have the shortest shafts and heaviest heads. Really they should be the easiest clubs in the set. The major difficulty is that the beginner knows that the ball is supposed to fly high with them and so starts to try to lift it into the air rather than allowing the loft of the club to do the work. Once one can talk oneself into letting the clubhead get the ball airborne, most of the difficulty is over.

The downward contact

The short irons can, in fact, be played in exactly the same way as the basic method for the medium irons, just brushing the grass on which the ball sits and letting the natural loft take over. However, if the lie is very good and grassy one tends to find that the ball may even float rather too high and lifelessly, without seeming to bore its way through the air. Rather than doing this, one begins to play these shots with a definite downward attack, taking the ball first, followed by a divot – the 'ball-turf contact' (Fig. 51). This has two advantages. Firstly, it means that one can hit the ball from both a good lie and a poor lie with much the same swing – useful because these clubs are essentially our recovery clubs too, and secondly it means that the ball travels with a crisper, more penetrating flight as the clubhead squeezes it out of the

51. With the short irons the attack on the ball has to be a definite downward one, taking the ball first and then a divot.

52–55. The swing with the short irons is essentially a short, compact one, with a downward attack into the back of the ball.

ground. Once you have hit a ball with a divot in this way you will appreciate the difference.

Achieving this difference in contact, squeezing it out, rather than brushing it away, is done partly by thinking of hitting *down* into the back of the ball, and partly by adjusting the stance. In dealing with the basic contact with the medium irons, the ball was placed to correspond to the bottom of the swing – for most women golfers just about the centre of the stance. But now we don't want to strike the ball at the bottom of the swing; we want to strike it before and behind the bottom of the swing. The ball is therefore positioned slightly further to the right in the feet, 2 inches or so behind the centre. The hands, however, hardly change position so they seem a little ahead of the clubhead (Fig. 52).

The swing

As the backswing takes place it is virtually the same as with the medium iron, perhaps stopping slightly shorter because one is concerned with control more than with distance. At the top of the backswing, then, the club shaft is not quite to the horizontal, the right leg is flexed, the grip is firm and, in fact, all the other rules of the backswing are adhered to (Fig. 53).

From the top of the backswing all the concentration must be on hitting down and staying down through the ball, trying to visualize the contact of the ball fol-

lowed by taking the divot. In the downswing the left heel must be most firmly pushed back to the ground and very definitely kept there, if anything slightly exaggerating the transference to the left foot. Now at impact the clubhead is most clearly travelling downwards, striking the ball and then continuing down to take quite a substantial divot (Fig. 54).

As the swing continues through impact the eyes are kept glued to the spot where the ball was, so that one can see that the divot has been taken. The weight is favouring the left foot rather more than it might have been with the basic medium iron shot and the left heel is firmly on the ground. Only as the swing finishes will the eyes come up to follow the flight of the ball, with the weight perfectly balanced, perhaps in a ratio of 70 to 30

between the left foot and right foot (Fig. 55).

The whole essence of hitting good short irons is to try for this downward 'ball-turf' contact, positioning the ball back in the feet very slightly, thinking of the type of contact you want and also concentrating on thrusting onto the left heel and foot in the downswing. The fault of the long handicap player is often that she tries to scoop the ball into the air and so actually falls onto the right foot through impact, with the left heel coming up. Try to resist the idea of lifting the ball but instead hit very much down into it.

The ball position

Here let me make a point for the better golfer. I have assumed in talking about the positioning of the ball that the bottom of the

54

55

from a few practice swings – simply moving the ball a couple of inches further to the right when you want a definite downward contact.

Stance and direction

One last point here for the experienced golfer. As you move the ball back in the feet the tendency is to meet up with it before the clubhead has reached its straight-through path, in other words while it is still travelling slightly from the inside. This is the reason why it is so easy to push a short iron shot to the right. Especially if the lie is poor one also tends to 'lean' on the ball a little, swaying slightly to the left to be sure of getting down to it, which exaggerates this even further. To strike the short irons on target it is therefore very often necessary to set the line of the feet slightly to the left of target, in technical terms, opening the stance. The amount one has to do this varies for the individual, and is largely a matter of trial and error and eventually a question of feel. The main point is to realize, however, that whenever the ball is played well back in the feet, this type of stance adjustment becomes necessary.

swing comes roughly opposite the middle of the feet. For the majority of women golfers, and certainly older golfers, this is the case. With the young single figure handicap player the bottom of the swing often comes slightly further to the left in the stance – usually the result of better leg work – so that the simple brushing contact at the bottom of the swing is usually achieved with the ball per-

haps one third of the way from the left foot to right, while the downward contact of the short irons is obtained with the ball still slightly ahead of the centre of the stance. Indeed, you will often see the tournament professional playing the ball well ahead of the centre of the stance for every shot. What is important is that one knows where the bottom of one's own swing comes – fairly obvious

The medium irons

The first five chapters really centred around learning a swing with the medium irons, just sweeping the ball away from the bottom of the swing. Then in the section on the short irons I looked at the type of 'ball-turf' contact one uses more correctly

with the short irons. With the medium irons one really has the choice. If the lie is really good, with a nice cushion of grass between the ball and solid ground, it is perfectly acceptable just to swish the ball away, clipping the grass rather than

taking a real divot. This is by far the easiest way for most club golfers to strike the ball.

However, when the lie is less good, the only way one gets a really crisp contact is by playing the ball fractionally further back in the stance, just as with the

short irons, and concentrating once again on hitting the ball on the downswing. This type of contact, where one strikes the ball with a divot, is perhaps considered the sounder and more solid method – the majority of professionals using it for every iron shot regardless of lie – but for the average woman golfer, if the lie permits, one is much better just to concentrate on sweeping it away fairly cleanly.

Adjust the contact with lie

The main point, then, with the medium irons is to decide which type of contact you want on the ball. Are you going to sweep the ball away, or do you need to squeeze it out with a divot? Having decided on this, position the ball accordingly. For the average woman golfer you can best sweep it away from around the centre of the stance, and

squeeze it out with a divot from about 2 inches further back in the feet. For the good player you can probably sweep it away from a few inches inside the left foot, and squeeze it out from just ahead of the centre of the stance. Having done this, concentrate completely on the contact you want with the ball, watching it well right through impact.

The long irons

The contact

When we move on to the long irons – the 2 (only a club for the good player), 3 and 4 – we really have the same type of choice. The ball can either be swept away from the bottom of the swing, just clipping the grass on which it sits, or it can be squeezed away by hitting the ball slightly on the downswing, followed by a small divot. For the average woman golfer and beginner there is really no choice to be made, however, for the second type of contact is decidedly difficult. If one decided to strike the ball with a divot and in turn moved it back in the feet, the chances are that the effective loft of the club would be decreased slightly, not producing either good height or carry on the shots. The ability to hit good long iron shots with a divot, essential when the lie is tight, only comes as the player begins to use better leg action and stronger hand action. Until one gets below about 18 handicap, then, the long irons, and especially the 3-iron, should only really be used when the lie

is quite good and one can sweep the ball away from the natural bottom of the swing. From a tight lie the 5-wood, as we will see later, is probably a better choice for the average woman golfer than the 3-iron.

As the player gets better and better, however, the hand action begins to get stronger so that the uncocking of the wrists naturally happens a little later in the swing. The leg action usually becomes faster too and the bottom of the swing starts to fall rather nearer the left foot. Now it is possible to play the ball rather ahead of the centre of the stance for the medium and long irons, giving maximum length and carry, but still being able to squeeze the ball away on the downswing. Let's look at my own action with the long irons, in this case a 3-iron from a comparatively tight lie.

The backswing and downswing

At address the stance is slightly wider than for the medium and short irons, giving a firmer base for the more powerful blow. The ball is positioned perhaps a third

of the way between the left and right foot (Fig. 56).

The backswing is full, with the wrists cocking freely, but the grip very firm. There always seems a real danger of the grip loosening with the long irons in particular, so take special note of this (Fig. 57).

From the top of the backswing the leg action largely dictates whether one can get the required contact. There must be a most definite and very active thrusting into the left heel, pulling both left knee and hip back as a result. The lower body is now very clearly ahead of the ball, while the speed of the left arm pull from the top of the backswing sees the wrists almost as fully cocked as they were at the top (Figs. 58 and 59).

Impact

At impact the hands are still fractionally ahead of the ball, giving it a firm, descending blow. The legs are still driving forward but the head is definitely behind the ball. An important point to note here is the firmness of the left arm and almost straight line down the arm and club shaft at impact (Fig. 60). It may be something of a well-worn golfing cliché, but I think the feeling of 'hitting against a firm left side' is most fitting. There is no buckling in the left arm or wrist and the left leg is firmly braced. It is largely the ability to get this driving action with the legs and firmness in the left arm which determines whether the woman golfer can achieve this downward contact with the long irons. The really good woman iron player will always be firmly on the left heel through impact, while exerting obvious pressure from the inside of the right foot, the heel just working off the ground.

The action beyond impact is vital. This is really the checkpoint one has in learning this contact. The eyes are focused on the spot where the ball was, so that it is clear whether one really has taken the divot, while the left leg is braced, heel down. The force of the impact works one almost towards the back and outside of the left foot so that it is common to see the toes slightly off the ground in this way. The left arm is still firmly in control, with the wrist unbroken, but just beginning to fold into the body while the right has at last fully straightened to give maximum width towards the target (Fig. 61).

The finish

Eventually the thrust generated into the left heel pulls the hips completely through so that at the end of the swing the left side is braced, the right relaxed, the body facing the target and the hands high and firmly in control of the club (Fig. 62).

56

57

60

61

58

59

62

56–62. The good golfer is able to play the ball a little further forward in the stance with the long irons, yet still hitting the ball with a slightly downward attack, taking a small divot beyond it.

The main points in beginning to achieve this type of crisp, solid contact with the ball are the tremendous speed generated in the pull down of the left arm, the driving action of the legs onto the left heel right through impact, a really firm grip throughout and lastly the concentration and determination that one really is going to stay down and see that divot taken.

The fairway woods

Although the scratch woman golfer and professional may only need to use a fairway wood three or four times in a round, for the average woman golfer the fairway woods are often the most used clubs in the bag. As a rule they are considerably easier to use than the long irons, partly, I am sure, because the larger heads look more powerful and so inspire confidence, and partly because the sweeping contact which one generally uses with the fairway wood requires less strength than the 'ball-turf' contact one needs to be a fine long iron player.

Let's look at the fairway woods. Firstly, the 2-wood, or 'brassie'. This has two distinct uses, either for the longer handicap player as an alternative to the driver, or, for the really good player in producing the most powerful shots from the fairway, particularly useful for boring into a head wind. Then comes the 3-wood, or 'spoon'. This is really the general purpose wood for gaining length along the fairway and is considerably easier for most club golfers than the 2-wood. The 4-wood, like the

3-wood, is a good general purpose club for achieving length, being perhaps 10 yards shorter than the 3-wood for the top-class player. For the average golfer the difference in distance between the two is probably less noticeable, while the 4-wood also has an advantage in being slightly easier to use. The 5-wood, which produces the highest and shortest shots of the four – about 180 yards for the top-class woman golfer – is an excellent alternative to the 2- and 3-irons, and also has tremendous possibilities in playing long semi-recovery shots from light rough or poor lies. So this is our set of woods. The 2 is primarily for the good golfer, the 3 and 4 are the general purpose clubs, and the 5 is both an alternative to the long irons and a good club to use from the rough. In technique, however, they are all tackled in much the same way.

From a good lie the ball is played in a position to correspond with the bottom of the swing – for the long handicap player just ahead of the centre of the stance, but for the good golfer gradually getting nearer the left heel. The stance is slightly wider than for the irons, giving firm balance, the backswing is full and unrushed, and the stress in the downswing is on sweeping the ball away, ensuring that the finish of the swing is both full and very, very firm (Figs. 63–68).

As the lie becomes less good the fairway woods can all be played in much the same way as the irons, playing the ball slightly further back in the feet and concentrating, not on a sweeping contact, but on a slightly downward one, taking the ball and then grazing the ground beyond. This is dealt with in more detail in Chapter 13.

The driver

63–68. With the fairway woods the swing is smooth and full, sweeping the ball away *en route* to a really good, long finish.

Although the saying is that 'one drives for show and putts for dough,' this is only really the case with top-class pro-

63

64

65

fessionals. Little separates world class players in any tournament but the extra telling putts they hole; their long game is virtually perfected. For the club golfer I am inclined to think that driving must be the most important part of the game. It is true that one can make up for the odd wayward shot by holing a good putt, but unless one gets a really high percentage of drives on the fairway good scoring is always a struggle. A good drive sets one up for the hole; a bad one demolishes every bit of confidence and with it your likelihood of scoring well.

The upward contact

For the longer handicap woman golfer I often think driving is the easiest part of the game. The ball is teed up, meaning that her natural instinct of hitting the ball slightly on the upswing, almost trying to scoop it into the air, is quite correct. However, once the player starts to hit good, crisp iron shots, taking the ball and then the divot, it is often hard to return to the idea of hitting the ball on the upswing. It is the idea of the contact one wants with the different types of shots which is the most important, first in learning good iron shots and then in striking the ball correctly with the driver.

In using the driver or 2-wood the ball should be teed up so that the top of the clubhead is just above the centre of the ball; this means that if swung reasonably correctly the clubhead cannot pass right under the ball. This tee height is important. Learn to tee the ball a consistent height and you are more likely to strike it the same every time. (One point for the beginner. In teeing the ball *don't* try to push the tee in the ground, and then perch the ball on top of it. Hold the ball on top of the tee and use this to push the tee down into the ground. Not only is it easier to get the ball to balance, but it is easier to judge the height correctly *and* it gives anyone watching the impression that you know what you are doing!)

Address and backswing

The idea is now to strike the ball on the upswing, in other words after the club has swung down to the bottom of the swing. To help produce this contact, the ball is positioned to the left of the natural bottom of the swing, opposite the left heel for our good golfer and about one third of the way from left foot to right for the longer handicap player

66

67

68

69. With the driver the attack on the ball is correctly an upward one, positioning the ball ahead of the natural bottom of the swing.

(Fig. 69). The stance is now at its widest, with the hands just about level with the ball, the shoulders, as always, square to the line of the shot and the right hand very much behind and not under the club in the grip (Fig. 70).

The club moves back low to the ground, perhaps delaying the wristcock slightly longer than with the irons. However, the right arm must still be allowed to fold neatly into the body, naturally bringing the clubhead back on the inside (Figs. 71 and 72). At the top of the backswing the shoulder turn is full, the club pointing straight down the line of the shot, with the hands firmly in control of the club and the left arm straight. The right leg is still in very much the same position it was at address with the knee flexed, while the left heel has pulled off the ground (Fig. 73).

Down and through

As the downswing starts, the left heel is pushed back to the ground very smartly, the left knee in turn beginning to straighten. Although the actual thrust into the heel is very marked that is not to say that all the weight is transferred to the left foot. At this stage the upper body is most definitely behind the ball, bringing the bottom of the swing where we want it. The legs then can be seen driving forwards while the head is held back, body arching (Figs. 74–76).

By the time impact is reached the upper body is still held well back so that the bottom of the swing has already been passed. The left heel, however, is still

70–81. With the driver the left heel is thrust firmly back to the ground in the throughswing but the body and back arch so that the whole mass of the body stays well behind the ball through impact, producing the right upward contact with it.

firmly planted on the ground. The eyes are focused most definitely on the back of the ball – the part you are hitting – while the left arm is swinging just as fast and freely as possible (Figs. 77 and 78).

Beyond impact the whole of the body is well behind where the ball was, the head if anything having moved slightly to the right through impact. Never to the left. The legs have worked on through, left fully braced, right knee towards the target. This idea of 'legs forwards, body back' is still very evident (Figs. 79 and 80).

The finish

As the swing is completed the weight distribution can be clearly seen. The thrust and pressure on the left heel has been very marked but the whole mass of the body has by no means moved entirely onto the left foot. Rather it is shared almost equally between the left foot and toes of the right. The back is arched, body facing down the fairway, with the hands high and the speed of the swing taking the club well down the back (Fig. 81).

The key points in hitting good drives are to position the ball ahead of the natural bottom of your swing, to stay behind the ball as you hit it – sweeping it upwards into the air, a really good grip in which the right hand is behind, *not* beneath, the shaft, and the confidence to accelerate right through to a firm, long, perfectly balanced finish.

7 PLAYING FROM SLOPING LIES

Standing above the ball

The shot where the ball is very much below one's feet is one of the most difficult for the club golfer. It exaggerates two of her most common weaknesses. Firstly, it tends to produce severely sliced shots and, secondly, it makes staying down to the ball all the more difficult. So it is not an easy one to tackle.

The main point in the stance is that the posture is naturally changed. The ball comes nearer to the feet while the body clearly has to bend over far more. This is something one just has to let happen and should not try either to produce or resist. This forces the shoulders to turn on a more upright plane, giving a higher backswing position (Fig. 82). From here, balance must be maintained while making a really conscious effort to stay down and watch the ball even longer than usual. This is perhaps the most difficult part of this situation for the club golfer. If she tends to look up under normal conditions, she is even more likely to do so here.

As far as the shot itself is concerned, this lie almost always leads to a slice. Don't fight this;

82. In standing above the ball the backswing becomes much more upright while the ball will always tend to drift away to the right in flight.

83. In standing below the ball the backswing becomes much flatter, tending to produce a shot which hooks away to the left. Compare the angle of the body and left arm between this and the action of Fig. 82

rather allow for it. Aim very well left of target, bearing in mind that the ground on which the ball lands is also likely to be sloping the same way. The ball will

not only curve to the right in the air but also kick further right on landing. So compensate for the slope and compensate sufficiently.

Standing below the ball

Standing above the ball tends to be more of a problem for the club golfer, exaggerating the likelihood of slicing. Conversely, standing below the ball is usually the more difficult for the better golfer; now it exaggerates any tendency to hook.

Again the slope of the ground forces a change in posture. With the ball somewhere approaching knee height, one is pushed further away from it, with the body held more erect. It is a good idea to shorten the grip on the club very slightly to minimize

this, but one cannot compensate for it entirely. The shoulders now tend to turn on a much more horizontal plane so that the swing flattens out (Fig. 83). This produces a shallow contact with the ball, leading to a rolling hooked shot which

84. With a downhill shot, weight must be pushed onto the left foot to bring the shoulders parallel with the slope of the ground, making a real effort to stay right down through the ball. The ball flies lower than usual and curves away to the right.

becomes much more severe with the degree of the slope. In this case the whole swing is once more adjusted to allow for this. The stance and clubface are set well right of the target, again taking into account that the ball is likely to be landing on ground sloping in the same direction, so both curving and kicking to the left. The good player can fight this to a degree by bringing the right hand onto the top of the club, in a slice grip, but as a rule it is much easier for most golfers to allow for the shot rather than try to prevent it.

Playing from a downhill lie

For the club golfer this is almost always more difficult than playing uphill. With this 'hanging lie' the main difficulty is to strike the ball cleanly without catching the

84

ground behind it. In order to get this good contact, the attack on the ball needs to be a very steep, downward one from a high, upright swing.

To encourage this steep attack, the ball has to be played very well back in the feet, the weight very much on the left so that the shoulders come virtually parallel with the slope. This enables the swing to travel up and then down the slope. However, in moving the ball back in the feet, two things happen which most definitely affect the flight of the ball. Firstly, the clubhead is tipped forwards, reducing the effective loft of the club. This means that the 5-iron will take up the characteristics of the 4 or even 3-iron, while the 3 and 4-woods become far too difficult for all but the tournament player. Secondly, the club tends to strike the ball before reaching its straight-through path and also before the clubface is square to the target. The ball therefore both starts to the right and drifts even further out there. The whole stance is therefore aimed very well to the left, making a real attempt to hit right down and through the ball and to follow the slope beyond impact (Fig. 84). In this situation never try to help the ball into the air; just take a more lofted club and trust it to get the ball up for you.

The long uphill shot

In playing uphill there are two main things which happen; the loft of the club tends to be exaggerated so that the 5-iron effectively becomes a 6-iron and secondly, the weight of the body gets thrown back onto the right foot. The first consideration is, therefore, that one has to be prepared to take plenty of club,

allowing both for the extra height and also for actually hitting up a hill which shortens the flight of the ball. One never need be afraid of taking a longer club uphill, for the extra height one gets means that the long irons and woods are at their easiest.

As far as the actual swing is concerned, we want to stand in

some way so that the clubhead can swing through without digging into the slope. With these long shots we are, after all, trying to sweep the ball away; we aren't trying to punch it away with a divot. The body is therefore set almost at right angles to the slope, weight naturally on the right foot, so that the swing

85. With a long uphill shot weight falls back onto the right foot at address, shoulders parallel with the slope, while the ball flies very high and pulls around to the left.

86. With a short shot from an uphill lie the swing can go into the slope, taking a solid divot. Weight is now kept on the left foot throughout, hitting into the slope through impact. Little difference in flight is then noticed.

85

86

can be just as normal but now following the line of the slope (Fig. 85). The tendency to be on the right foot through impact produces a shot which tends to both pull and curve away to the left. Rather than trying in any way to correct this, one should allow for this by aiming the whole shot – the clubface, the stance and the whole swing – to the right of target.

Short irons from uphill lies

The short irons, and for the good golfer the medium irons, can be tackled in a very different way from the longer shots in this kind of situation. With these shots we can now punch the ball away with a divot so that it doesn't matter if the through-swing goes rather into the slope. With the long irons and woods we had to swing up the slope to sweep the ball away; now we can swing more into the slope. In this case, the body can be held vertically so that the left leg necessarily bends and weight is set towards it. In the backswing the weight is kept very much on the left foot, maintaining this right through impact. With the ball again well forward in the feet the downswing can be made very firm – down and right through the ball and then the turf (Fig. 86). In this case very little difference in flight is noticed. In fact the most likely tendency is to push the ball to the right if one exaggeratedly sways through onto the left foot. So here we are hitting into the hill, not up it – a shot which the good player can extend to the medium and even the long irons. For the average woman golfer it is more the shot for the 7 or 8-iron upwards.

8 A CHAPTER FOR THE SLICER

What makes golf difficult?

To the ordinary club player, golf often seems an absurdly difficult game. The swing seems unnatural and illogical, and the ball has the uncanny habit of doing just the opposite of what you want. The underlying difficulty is that it is a game of spin and curves; the ball doesn't easily fly straight. If I throw a ball it travels in the direction in which I throw it. It doesn't suddenly curve off to right or left for no reason. Therefore if I throw a ball to a target and it consistently goes to the left I can adjust my throw quite naturally by attempting to throw it a little more to the right.

The golf ball, however, doesn't act in this way. Direction in the golf swing has two distinct factors; firstly, we have the initial direction in which it travels, corresponding to the natural instincts of throwing a ball, but secondly, we have the way in which it curves. It is the distinction between the two which the club golfer usually fails to make. She simply doesn't understand the way in which the ball reacts.

The average club golfer slices; because she sees the ball travel out to the right her mind goes back to the instinct which tells her how to adjust the direction in which the ball is thrown. So immediately she strives to aim the whole swing more to the left in an effort to hit the ball straight. Instead she purely aggravates the slicing problem. In golf the two factors need to be treated entirely separately. A ball which curves to the right is by no means the same as the one which goes straight out to the right. The ball curves because swing and clubface are mis-aligned. It is basically the fact that the clubface is directed to the right of the direction of the swing which makes the ball curve out to the right (Fig. 87). In turn it is the direction of the swing which controls the way in which the ball starts. Try to separate the ideas of the two – the initial direction of the shot is the one which corresponds to the idea of throwing a ball. Any curve on the shot is a question of the alignment of the clubface, often associated with grip problems, and cannot be corrected instinctively. Before you ever start to correct a faulty flight in your shots, analyse this pattern carefully in terms of both initial direction and curve spin so that you really do know what type of fault you are dealing with.

The slice is born

Most golfers just beyond the real beginner's stage fall into one of two contrasting categories; they either hit the ball low and to the left through a faulty grip or, if the grip is relatively sound, they slice it out to the right. Those who fall into the second of these classes have a task in hand. Almost everything one needs to do to eliminate the slice is entirely opposite to instinct. The slicer, although she appreciates that the ball is curving away to the right, treats it as though it were simply flying straight there. The more she tries to steer it to the left, the more it swerves away to the right.

The slice is caused by spin being put on the ball and the spin in turn is put on by cutting across the line of the shot. This happens in one of two ways. Either the clubface is left looking out to the right at impact – the 'open clubface' – or the swing is aimed very much left of target with the clubface roughly on target. The important point is that the direction of the two is in opposition. The swing goes to the left and the clubface to the right.

What usually sets the golfer *en route* to being a slicer is that her hands and arms are relatively weak when it comes to whipping the clubhead through the ball. She gets no 'swish' at impact. The clubface is therefore left pointing out to the right as the ball is struck, sending it curving away to the right. If the professional can catch the pupil at this stage the damage is relatively easy to put right. However, all too often the golfer continues without professional advice and very naturally starts trying to steer the ball back to the left. Now not only is her clubface pointing to the right but the swing is going to the left and the perfect picture of the slicer is created – the left-aimed or 'out-to-in' swing combined with the right-aimed or 'open' clubface.

SWING

CLUBFACE

88

89

90

88. Incorrect. The clubface can often be returned to the ball in an open position if the turn through of the arms is blocked. At impact the elbow joint points to the target, the arm eventually buckling in the followthrough and the clubface looking straight upwards.

89 and 90. Correctly the action of the arms and clubface is mirrored in the backswing and throughswing. The right elbow points downwards in the backswing as it begins to fold into the body while the left elbow should point downwards halfway through the followthrough as it too begins to fold away.

Beginning to correct the slice

The main point in correcting the slice is to get both the clubface and the line of the swing aimed in the same direction at impact. As a rule the clubface is the easier of the two to tackle first. We want to enable the hands to bring the clubface squarely to the ball. This

87. The slice is caused by misdirecting the clubface and swing. Basically the clubface is aimed to the right with the swing travelling to the left of it, imparting a slice spin onto the ball.

either involves a correction in the grip – ensuring that the 'V's between thumb and index finger of both hands point to the right shoulder and not to the chin – or training the hands and wrists to work freely and swish the clubhead through impact.

The most common fault in the grip, I suppose, is in letting the right hand slip exaggeratedly under the club, but in the slicer's grip just the reverse is done. She now let's the left hand get under the club and folds the right hand over too far, so

that the 'V' between the thumb and index finger points to the chin or even left of it. What now happens is that by the time the clubhead is returned to impact, the right hand comes through very much behind the shaft and not on top of it, in turn twisting the club to an open position, where it faces off to the right with exaggerated loft (Figs. 12 and 13). This sends the ball off with too much height, weakly curving away to the right.

To correct this, the hands

need to be turned more to the right on the club so that the 'V's of both hands go much closer to the right shoulder. However, although in theory the further and further right these 'V's get even beyond the shoulder the more one improves a slice, this doesn't always happen in practice and I would be very hesitant about letting the 'V's actually get outside the right shoulder.

Using the hands and arms

Once the grip is correct, the hands need to be trained to produce more and more 'swish' through the ball and also to bring the clubface in perfectly squarely. Firstly, one can develop the right type of 'swish' by practising with the feet together, immobilizing the leg and body action and *making* the hands do the work.

Secondly, the actual way in which the hands and arms work through impact needs to be looked at in rather more detail. What very often happens is that in the downswing the left arm stays straight, as it should, but straight in an incorrect and very vulnerable way. As it reaches impact the elbow bone points out towards the target, with the face very often – if one could only stop the action on camera – in an open position. Beyond impact the left arm either buckles at the elbow or collapses at the wrist while the right takes over. The clubface now looks almost directly upwards as it reaches hip or waist height (Fig. 88). What should happen is that through impact the left arm gradually turns, so that the elbow bone begins to point downwards. The arm now starts to fold very smoothly into the body just as the right did in the backswing so that there is no sudden buckling (Figs. 89 and 90). Now as the club reaches this hip-height position, the elbow is pointing downwards, the right arm is able to stay extended and the back of the right hand faces away from the body. The toe of the club is now brought into a position where it points almost directly upwards. This mirrors almost exactly what happens in the backswing so that in the intermediate position through impact the clubface is likely to be square, or very nearly square. The left arm, then, needs to be firmly in control, turning through impact so that it can fold smoothly into the side, and allowing the clubface to square up through impact.

Tackling the swing

Once the hands are active and the grip is correct, the next stage is to direct the swing on target. This is the more difficult part of improving and eliminating the slice. The player who slices is naturally afraid of the right side of the course, and yet it is the fact that she tries to direct the swing very much to the left which brings about the slice in the first place. She is in effect cutting across the ball.

Hitting from the 'inside'
What one has to do is to encourage the player to attack the ball from the 'inside' – in other words so that she feels that the swing is travelling through in a right-aimed direction (Fig. 91). For the player who is forever in the trees and bushes on the right, this isn't an easy thing to develop. Naturally it feels both uncomfortable and quite contrary to have to attack the ball with the idea of hitting it out to the right. Indeed, the first experimental stages of this usually do produce shots which finish even further to the right – now both starting there and slicing away even further – but with well supervised teaching the more the player can talk herself into hitting out to the right the straighter the shots will fly. She is gradually learning to get swing and clubface in the right direction.

The stance
As a start, the whole direction of the stance very often needs to be changed. The slicer often assumes an open position in the way she stands to the ball, with either the feet or the shoulders turned towards the target and so left-aimed. This, quite naturally, is her way of feeling she can

INSIDE

OUTSIDE

91

92

93

91. The clubhead should always attack the ball from the inside, from there travelling through to the target and then returning inside once more. The slicer tends to attack the ball from the outside in a feeling of steering the ball to the left. To get the right attack on the ball from the inside she will probably have to feel that the whole downswing is directed well right of target.

92. Incorrect. If the turn of the shoulders is insufficient the club points left of target and the whole downswing follows this pattern, attacking the ball from the outside.

93. Incorrect. Instead of generating speed in the downswing with the left arm, swinging it away from the right shoulder, the slicer tends to deliver power with the right arm and shoulder, bringing the body round and attacking the ball from the outside.

94. In the correct action of attacking the ball from the inside the right shoulder is very passive in the change of directions, swinging the left arm freely down and away from it.

keep the ball to the left. What she may not appreciate is that the clubface and line of the swing are immediately set at odds with one another and the perfect slice is a virtual certainty. The remedy is to keep the clubface aimed on target, but to ensure that the line of the feet, hips, and particularly the shoulders points down the line of the shot or even fractionally right of it.

In theory if one closes the stance, in other words directing it to the right but with the club face on target, this should help the player attack the ball from the 'inside' and so eliminate the slice. In some cases this is sufficient. But if one overdoes the closing of the stance the player often feels awkwardly aimed to the right and resists this by turning the shoulders into the shot even more. However, if the slicer can learn to withdraw the right foot slightly at address into a closed position and then follow the line of the stance in the downswing, the swing can gradually be directed on target.

Aiming in the backswing

With the set-up correctly aimed, let's move on to the backswing. Like the address position the purpose of this is very much one of aiming the whole swing on target. The degree to which one turns the shoulders has an enormous bearing on the direction in which the club points at the top of the backswing. This in turn largely controls the direction of the downswing. If the shoulders are turned quite freely the back should be fully facing the target, the club pointing straight down the fairway. However, for a number of reasons it is very easy not to get this full turn. This happens if the left heel is kept anchored. It can happen very easily with the older golfer who isn't supple in the back or it can happen if one just hasn't got the confidence to turn away from the ball. In this case the backswing becomes aimed very much to the left of the target (Fig. 92). This almost invariably aims the downswing in this same direction, once again set-ting the directions of the swing and clubface in opposition. So the turn has to be full and unrestricted, giving the left heel the freedom to pull fractionally off the ground, and so pointing the club in the right direction for the downswing.

Lead down with the left

Once the backswing is correctly aimed, the next crisis point for the slicer usually comes in the order in which the downswing begins. This must be started with the thrusting down of the left heel and pulling down of the left arm. For most golfers using the left side in this way doesn't come naturally; it is the right side – in particular the shoulder – in which strength can be felt. So in an attempt to hit the ball hard the right shoulder tends to initiate the change of directions, turning the whole body into the shot before the arms have ever had time to start their swing down. By the time the club reaches impact the body has unwound itself almost fully to the target, throwing the swing into a left-aimed direction (Fig. 93). This does one of two things; it either produces a pull straight left, particularly with the shorter irons, or, if the hand action is slow, it leads to a slice, starting well left but swerving off to the right.

What the slicer needs to feel is that from the top of the backswing the right shoulder is held back, while the left arm swings as fast and freely away from it as possible (Fig. 94). One of the best ways of developing this action is to practise swinging with the left arm; building up left arm control helps to minimize the forcing action of the right side of the body, and in turn directs the swing on target.

Ideas to help you

The main reason why the slice is a problem is that the player simply doesn't understand what the shot is. The ball is not flying straight right. It curves out there because basically the swing goes to the left, with the clubface to the target or the right of it, and so putting a spin onto the ball. To eliminate this spin, swing and clubface must be aimed in the same direction. The slice tends to be caused by a poor grip – with the 'V's to the chin or left shoulder – or more commonly by slow, stiff hand and wrist action through the ball. It is then aggravated by trying to steer the ball to the left through setting the feet and shoulders to the left, or by throwing in power with the right side of the body. To eliminate the slice actually try to develop a hook situation, by aiming the clubface to the left and the swing to the right. Feel that you attack the ball very much from the inside while exaggeratedly rolling the right hand over the left to close the clubface. Once one can feel a hooked ball – and it is a very different feeling – it is very much easier to realize just what a slice is and so to correct it.

9 OTHER LONG GAME FAULTS

The low hooked shot

Two main problems of the woman golfer – hooking the ball and getting poor height and carry – are very much associated. The problem is almost entirely one of the grip. In this fault the right hand is very much under the shaft, with the 'V' between thumb and index finger probably not even visible, or certainly pointing outside the right shoulder. The left hand in turn is usually well on top of the shaft, with all four knuckles showing (Fig. 10). In the downswing the right hand and wrist turn through so that the right hand is behind and not beneath the shaft. In turn the clubhead is twisted into the closed, left aimed, position (Fig. 11).

This closed clubface position does two things. Firstly it has the tendency to send the ball curving away to the left, but secondly it tends to produce very poor height and carry. The effective loft of the clubface is reduced. The 8-iron produces shots with the trajectory of the 6-iron, the 6-iron produces the height of a 4-iron and so on. With the shorter irons this is a very small problem, and the player often seems strong and powerful with these clubs. However, once one gets to the 3-iron the loft often becomes reduced to that of a 1-iron, and it takes a very good player to even get the ball airborne with this club! With the woods the same is true. The player can sometimes hit quite good shots with the 5-wood from the fairway, and perhaps the 3-wood from the tee, but once she gets to the driver there is little chance of producing much flight to the ball. It is the loss of height which is often more noticeable to the woman golfer than the actual hook. But the two are closely connected.

Checking the 'V's in the grip

To produce good height and carry to the shots and eliminate the tendency to hook the ball, the right hand has to be behind and *not* underneath the club in the grip. It is now likely to come through impact with the hand in the same position it started, returning the clubface squarely. First of all the left hand must be correct – the 'V' pointing inside the right shoulder, about three knuckles showing and the thumb pulled close to the index finger. The important point from here is to feel the club rests in the fingers of the right hand and not the palm. The right hand can then be folded well over the left, covering the thumb, and bringing the 'V' so that it points inside the right shoulder.

This change is not always easy to make. To the player who hits the ball rather low, having the right hand very much under the club gives the impression of somehow being able to get under the ball and so lift it into the air. The player often makes the necessary change in the grip at address but then lets it slip back, right hand underneath, before starting the swing. This easily happens in waggling the club back and through a couple of times or tightening and loosening the grip in the address. So the grip needs to be checked once more just before the takeaway. I think the easiest way to realize the true bearing the grip has on the height one produces, is to exaggerate putting the right hand over – even letting the 'V' point left of the chin. If one can once do this and produce a high shot which drifts away to the right, it is much easier to convince oneself that the change really does need to be made.

The good golfer's hook

It is often said that the hook is the fault of the good golfer. Certainly the type of hook in my second category is only likely to strike the better player. In this, it is not so much the clubface alone which is in the wrong position at impact, but the direction of the swing which may be at fault. Whenever a ball hooks the clubface looks to the left of the line of the swing. In the hooker's grip one is mainly concerned with the faulty direction of the clubface. However, one can just as easily produce a hook if the clubface is aimed on target but the swing to the right. Once more the two are mis-directed in relation to one another; this time the ball starting out to the right but hooking back to the left.

This is generally produced in one of two ways. The first is one of the set-up, allowing the feet and body to be aimed off to the right, with the clubface roughly on target. This 'closed stance' immediately sets the direction of the swing and clubface at odds with one another (Fig. 17). This, of course, is instinctive to the player who already hooks. She sees the ball swerve away to the left and so counteracts this, she assumes, by aiming the feet more to the right. In reality all she does is to aggravate the hooking problem by mis-directing swing and clubface even more.

The second way of producing the true hook which starts out to the right and bends back to the left, is to restrict the turn through of the body while producing a very fast arm action. At impact the line of the swing is forced out to the right, while the arms may have to scissor and fold away too quickly by being hampered by lack of turn through of the body. This gives the really classic hook – an 'in-to-out' swing combined with a rapidly closing clubface. This produces shots which start well out to the right, sometimes curving back the whole width of the fairway to finish in the rough on the left. The real danger of this action is that it becomes even worse if slightly mis-timed. The more the golfer tries to steer the ball the more likely the arms are to scissor and so the quicker the clubface closes. The real answer here is to speed up the turn through of the body so that the line of the swing is brought through on target and not to the right of it. At the same time the left arm needs very definite training so that it can stand up to the speed of the right through impact, without collapsing and letting the clubface close. The checkpoint for this is a full followthrough in which the body faces the target, the left arm in perfect control and swinging at maximum speed right through to the followthrough.

The topped shot

Let's move on from the fault which only affects the really good woman golfer to the one which causes most trouble to the real beginner. This is the topped shot where the ball just runs along the ground.

One of the main reasons for producing this is from purely misunderstanding how the ball should rise. Instead of letting the natural loft of the club do the work, the player tries to scoop the ball into the air. This causes her to fall back on the right foot through impact, with the club-head brushing the ground behind the ball and then coming up and almost over it – catching the very top of the ball (Fig. 48). The point for the beginner to realize is that one cannot get under the ball – except when it is teed up for the drive. To get the ball airborne one must get to the bottom of it, but it is correctly a downward and not an upward attack. If the player can realize this and accentuate the effort to get onto the left foot through impact, making this even more pronounced the worse the lie, she should have little trouble in getting the ball into the air.

The second reason the beginner produces topped shots is that she tends to look at the top of the ball instead of the back of it – the part one is trying to hit. If one looks at the top of the ball – either at address or by moving the eyes during the swing – one tends to hit the top of the ball; if one looks at the back of it then there is more chance of hitting the back.

The third important cause of topping the ball is tension. This is more the fault of the medium handicap player. She may not normally top a shot in practice, but under the pressure of competition or playing in front of people the topped shot sometimes shows up. Through being tense she breathes in suddenly

95. Incorrect. Where the downswing is not started with the correct pull down of the left arm, the wrists tend to uncock prematurely, bringing the clubhead down behind the ball and producing a fluffed shot. This can also happen if the grip loosens during the swing.

95

and deeply and the whole rib cage seems to lift. This shortens the radius of the swing and means that she either may not get back to the bottom of the ball or may catch it right off the toe of the club. The lesson to be learned is to have a really good, relaxed practice swing, feeling the limbs to be loose and free and the breathing to be smooth. Then in the swing keep from forcing the shot and pay more attention to watching the ball really well than to anything else.

The fluffed shot

In the fluffed shot the clubhead chops into the ground behind the ball, instead of correctly taking a divot beyond it. In technical terms this is basically the result of 'hitting early'. What this really means is that in the change of directions at the top of the backswing the arms do not start down correctly as a unit with the wrists remaining cocked, but that at the start of the downswing there is an uncocking of the wrists. In the correct action the wrists are still well cocked halfway through the downswing (Fig. 75) and the clubhead only passes the hands after the ball has been struck (Fig. 80). To a certain degree women always have to hit slightly earlier than men, less strength in the wrists meaning that they have to uncock more gradually and rather sooner in the downswing. For this reason one often sees virtually top class women golfers rising up onto the toes through impact to make way for an earlier hit. But where the downswing is initiated almost entirely with an uncocking action of the wrists they become fully uncocked before reaching the ball, catching the ground several inches behind it (Fig. 95).

This happens in one of two ways. Firstly the left arm may be weak. Instead of pulling down from the top of the backswing, the right hand throws the club out from the top, losing the wristcock and straightening the wrists almost immediately. It is important to stress here the need to develop a fast change of direction with the left arm, swinging the club up and down with the left arm alone. Now the wrists can naturally enter impact in a slightly cocked position.

The second reason, and the one which is likely to produce an odd fluffed shot rather than a definite pattern of fluffed shots, is for the grip to loosen at the top of the backswing. The start of the downswing now sees the hands regripping the club and once again destroying the wristcock too early. Once more the clubhead is brought down behind the bottom of the ball. This is perhaps most likely to happen with the long irons, where the length of the shaft often pulls the left hand open at the top of the backswing.

96. Incorrect. The ball tends to be pushed out to the right of target when the turn through of the body is incomplete. The left leg has not become braced and the whole finish gives the appearance that the shot has been aimed well right.

96

The pushed shot

The pushed shot – the one where the ball flies straight out to the right – is often closely associated with the hook. The fault once again is in the direction of the attack on the ball, once more the line of the swing going out to the right of the target. With the hooked shot the hands then turn to close the clubface while in the pushed shot the clubface aims out along the line of the swing.

What commonly happens is that players hook with the driver and other longer clubs but then push the ball with the short irons. A very common cause of the push is for the unwinding of the body through impact to be slow and incomplete. The left leg often remains bent instead of becoming braced in the downswing so that the left hip does not turn out of the way as it should. The whole body is then left looking very obviously out to the right at the finish of the swing with the club striking the ball in an in-to-out (right-aimed) direction (Fig. 96). The correction here is to work on a definite clearing through of the left hip, ensuring that there is a good thrust into the left heel to start the downswing, straightening the left knee and bracing the left leg as the swing changes directions.

A second major cause of pushing the ball to the right is striking it before the club has reached its straight through path, caused by the body being too far ahead of the ball at impact. This can either happen if the ball is simply played too far back in the feet or if there is a distinct lateral sway to the left in the downswing. Either way the club is still travelling in a right-aimed direction at impact and the ball will start well right of target.

The shank or socket

The shank or socket – the shot where the ball flies off the neck of the iron club and out to the right – is one of the awful shots of golf. What makes it even more frightening is that the more one resists it the worse it tends to become.

The difficult thing about writing about socketing is that there are so many ways of doing it – often quite opposite to one another. One can naturally socket through standing too close to the ball and simply not having room to swing the arms through, or one can socket through standing too far from the ball and reaching for it. One can socket from an exceptionally in-to-out swing, in which the hands do not work through, or one can socket through swinging from out-to-in. Indeed, I have had the occasional beginner who could only strike the ball on the clubface and not the shaft by trying to miss it on the inside. Here the fault is simply bad co-ordination. So the socket is a difficult fault to diagnose in any general terms.

Two common causes

The two main faults I would say, however, are these: swinging around from the outside and blocking the hands from an in-to-out path. The first of these is usually associated with smothered drives, dragging them straight round to the left, or catching the ball off the heel of the club. The fault here is one of being very dominant with the right arm and hand. From the top of the backswing the downward action is initiated incorrectly with the shoulders, showing a marked loop in the path so that the clubhead gets well outside the line. If the hands work rather slowly the player is likely to slice, but if they work at speed the clubface is closed on the ball with the neck coming in to meet it. The remedy here is very much like that of the slice, working on getting the clubhead to attack the ball from the inside. A good exercise for this type of socket is to put two balls side by side an inch apart and to try to hit the one closer to you, leaving the other in place.

The second fault is the one which can happen suddenly and then get worse and worse the more one thinks about it. The problem here is that the player approaches impact with the wrists fully cocked and then does not release them in the impact zone to cross over in the followthrough as they should. Instead the clubface is left wide open and the neck brought to the ball. The unfortunate point here is that as the socket is so disastrous, having done it once one is likely to ease up on the next shot. In easing up, the clubface is again left wide open, making the chance of socketing even greater. This type of shot is particularly likely to arise with half shots – slightly less than full 8-, 9- or 10-irons – when the swing is less than full speed and the use of the hands is not essential. For the player who sockets in this way, the important point is to be brave enough to hit through with the hands on every shot. The more inhibited one is, the more likely one is to socket. So hit hard and release the hand action through the ball.

Lack of distance

For the average woman golfer maximum length is one of the essentials for improving the overall game. With men's golf length from the tee is rarely indicative of handicap, but for women golfers most of the handicap is simply taken up with not being able to reach the greens in the required number. With women's golf take the longest hitters in a club and you nearly always have the best players. So length is, or should be, the chief aim of the vast majority of women golfers.

One of the main points is to have the right idea of hitting the ball hard. It requires physical effort to hit the ball a long way. Too many women golfers simply swing slowly and gently at the ball and then expect it to travel a couple of hundred yards. Well, it won't. All the advice about swinging the club easily and smoothly is fine for the majority of men who have a natural ability to hit the ball hard. For them one almost has to curb the tendency to hit the ball too hard while trying to develop a swing for good direction. But, providing the woman golfer can look at the ball well through impact and can maintain good balance in the throughswing, she can work and work on really attacking the ball with ferocity. A lazy, gentle swing will not produce maximum length. It requires effort.

In the actual technique of the swing it is largely the action of the hands, wrists and arms which determine the type of length one can achieve. In the backswing the wrists must cock fully, the club being supported at the top of the swing by the left thumb. The grip on the club must be perfectly firm, without any opening of the left hand on the club, from here really pulling down with the left arm at maximum speed and then throwing the clubhead at the ball with the hands. At the same time the left heel is pushed back to the ground, feeling a distinct pressure in the left heel while the leg begins to be braced. It is this which starts the change in direction of the body action, multiplying the force generated by the hands and arms alone. The whole aim of the downswing should be to generate speed, not just hitting at the ball, but really working through quite uninhibitedly from the top of the backswing to a really long, full, balanced followthrough.

Achieving distance requires perfect timing, but it also requires sheer physical effort and a determination to hit the ball really hard.

Difficulty with driving

In the medium handicap range, say about 8 to 18, it is fairly common to find players who have become quite good with the irons and fairway woods, but who find great difficulty with driving. Usually the player produces a good, downward contact with the irons, also hits her fairway woods slightly on the downswing, almost with a divot, but then finds it very difficult to adjust to the right type of upward, sweeping contact with the driver. The only way this type of player can play good drives is in teeing the ball very low, using a driver or 2-wood, and almost hitting it in the same way as the fairway wood. As a rule, though, the shot takes up rather too much backspin and doesn't travel as far as one would expect. It lands softly and gets very little run. From a normal height of tee, the shot often comes off the top of the clubhead with exceptional height.

For this player the upward contact of the driver which the beginner finds so easy is the hardest part of the game. The exercise here is to tee the ball up fairly high and well forward in the stance and to learn to hit it on the upswing, preferably using a driver rather than a 2-wood. For this player the problem is that as she moves the ball forward in the stance so she adjusts the whole swing, bringing the bottom of the swing right to the ball instead of behind it and so hitting it like an iron (Fig. 97). Correctly the ball should be moved forwards in the stance, but with the bottom of the swing still falling in the same place as it does with the irons and so roughly opposite the middle of the feet. The clubhead should just graze the grass behind the bottom of the ball and then

97. Incorrect. The medium handicap golfer often produces a downward attack on the ball with the driver, just as one should with the irons. The ball is often actually caught from the top of the clubhead. The fault here is that the weight has swayed onto the left foot and so ahead of the ball by impact.

98. The correct feeling with the driver must be one of attacking the ball from behind, so that the bottom of the swing falls opposite the middle of the stance, continuing on to collect the ball on the upswing.

brush it away on the upswing.

To learn to do this, focus the eyes on a spot on the ground where the ball would be, roughly opposite the left heel. Then practise swinging so that the clubhead brushes the ground some 6 inches behind this spot. In doing this, keep the eyes focused on the spot where the ball would be, *not* at the point where you want to touch the ground. To start with, the contact is likely to be too steep and chopping, so gradually this contact needs to become shallower and shallower. To produce this, the centre of gravity of the body must stay well behind the ball right through impact, *not* falling back off the left heel as the longer handicap often does, but by arching the body and back in the down and throughswing (Fig. 98). The legs, then, are very active, with the left heel firmly on the ground, but the head is kept very much behind the ball. The feeling must be one of hitting the ball away from you – from behind – and not one of swaying onto it. The result is a follow-through in which the left heel is flat on the ground, left leg braced, but with plenty of weight balanced on the toes of the right. If done correctly, the player is more likely to fall back on the right foot than to sway forwards onto the left.

INCORRECT

97

10 AROUND THE GREEN

Learning to chip and pitch

Obviously when we get closer to the green we get to a point where we can no longer use a full shot. Even a full shot with a sand wedge will travel about 40 yards for the newer golfer. So now we have to learn a variety of shorter shots. These basically fall into two classes – the pitch shot and the chip shot. The pitch shot is used when one has to lob the ball over some obstacle, perhaps a bunker, a bank or strip of thick grass. For this shot one uses one of the most lofted clubs – the 10-iron (or pitching wedge) or the sand wedge. The idea is to produce a high shot which carries over the trouble and then rolls perhaps 5 yards as it lands on the green. The second shot, the chip, is used where there is no obstacle to negotiate. This is a lower shot, played with a medium iron, just carrying a couple of yards and then running most of the way.

The basic method of learning both the chip shot and the pitch shot is much the same. It is the choice of clubs which really dictates the exact shot produced. So let's start with a 6- or 7-iron, first learning the basic action of the chip and from there moving on to the pitch.

Training firmness

The underlying fault of the beginner when she starts to learn both chipping and pitching is that she tries to scoop the ball into the air by flicking the clubhead at it with her wrists. The left arm stops at impact, the wrists collapse and the clubhead catches the top of the ball, just sending it scuttling along the ground (Fig. 99). What she

lacks is the necessary firmness through the ball. The good player, by contrast, has the back of the left wrist and forearm in a perfectly straight line through impact, relying on the loft of the club to produce the required shot (Fig. 100).

So the first stage to good chipping is to train firmness in the left arm. Because this solid action through the ball is so unnatural for the beginner, one has to adopt an address position in which the firmness and control is already there (Fig. 101). The arms are held straight and rather wooden with the hands

99. Incorrect. The fault of the long handicap golfer is that she tries to scoop the ball into the air, the left arm stopping at impact and the wrist collapsing.

99

and wrists firmly locked in position. In the swing this whole unit of arms and club is going to move as one – a pendulum action from the shoulders with no breaking of the wrists. The second of our aims in the address is to produce a small, delicate swing. The ball hasn't got to travel far. So the club is gripped well down the shaft, the shorter the shot the further down towards the end of the grip one can hold. This immediately gives one more control of the clubhead and, after all, in little shots like this it is control not power that is needed. The third thing we are concerned with here is making it just as easy as possible to hit the ball to the flag. In the long game, although this is one of the aims, we are also concerned with winding up in the backswing to generate power. We therefore have to adopt a square stance – parallel to the line of the shot – to enable the body to turn to create this energy. In the short game this isn't necessary. Here, then, we can turn a little towards the target in very much the same way one would in throwing a ball under-arm to a target. The feet are therefore turned a little towards the flag, 6 or 9 inches apart, so that the knees too point slightly in this direction, flexing them and concentrating the weight a little on the left foot.

The pendulum action

The swing is now purely a pendulum type of swing from the shoulders, with the left arm and clubshaft in a straight line right the way through. Backswing and throughswing are of identical

101

102

103

length, with the hips turning slightly both ways – the left knee pointing in behind the ball on the backswing and the right knee to the target on the throughswing (Figs. 102 and 103). The whole essence here is the firmness at the ball, the rigidity of the left arm and the straight line position of the club and arm beyond impact. Compare Figures 99 and 103 to see how in the correct action the left arm has kept moving through impact so that the wrists have not collapsed. If the left arm stops at or before the ball, the right hand is forced to come past the left, giving the loose, flicking action which typifies the beginner.

To develop the right action and correct firmness one needs to stress the co-ordination of two movements in the through-

swing – the left arm working at a steady, continuous pace through impact with the right knee being eased on through towards the target as the heel pulls its way off the ground. This enables the whole action to stay very smooth and the club to travel out towards the hole. So practise co-ordinating the two – left arm through, right knee through – as the basis of your whole chipping action.

Pitching is essentially just the same as chipping. However, the extra loft of the wedges means that one has to take a rather bigger swing for a pitch shot of a given length than for a chip, more of the power being taken up in producing height. The pitch can be adapted right the way from a little shot over a bank by the green up to very nearly a

101–103. The beginner must adopt a very wooden address position, setting the left arm and club in a very firm, straight line and holding well down the club for better control. The swing is a pendulum action from the shoulders, keeping the arms and club moving as a unit without any breaking of the wrists on either backswing or throughswing.

full shot, gradually producing a bigger and bigger action to give a longer shot. In the end one therefore gets to a point where the wrists have to break in the backswing, somewhere around shoulder height, to produce the required length (Fig. 104). The whole action must still be firm, however, with the wrists solid through impact and the finish showing the left arm having moved well through and in control of the club (Fig. 105).

Judging the shot

100. In the correct action the back of the left wrist is perfectly firm and the arm is kept moving right through impact.

The first thing to decide in playing to the green is just which type of shot you need. Do you

need to pitch the ball over something onto the green, or is the ground smooth enough that you

104

105

104 and 105. Only with a longer pitch shot do the wrists eventually need to break but the emphasis is still on a stiff, wooden action.

can run it all the way? Don't get caught between the two. Either pitch it well to the flag with a wedge or run it with the 6- or 7-iron.

With a pitch shot I invariably use my sand wedge. After all I want to get a high shot so why not use the most lofted club available? I then look at the shot and pick out a spot where I want the ball to land, say 5 yards in front of the flag. From here I forget about the hole and just concentrate on dropping the ball on this spot. With a running shot, by contrast, I try to judge the whole length of the shot without being concerned where the ball lands, using a 7-iron for almost all chipping. In exceptional circumstances I may move to a 6- or even 5-iron on a very long green, and use the 8 or 9 if the flag is close to the edge of the green but the fairway thick and lush. On the whole, however, I think it is very much better to choose two definite clubs for your short game, the 6 and sand wedge or 7 and sand wedge, learning to master these before venturing onto anything else.

Swing length controls distance

Having got a good picture of the shot you are playing, the important point is how hard to hit the ball. At first, of course, this is largely a process of trial and error. One is just trying to associate the size or strength of swing with the distance the ball travels. The way in which one controls the length of the shot, however, is most important. It is the length of the swing which must control the length of the shot, not a drastic change in speed. So as the shot gets longer, so the swing must get longer – both backswing *and* throughswing – but keeping the firmness in the left arm through the ball.

As a rule, it is shortening rather than lengthening the original action which is more of a problem. The older golfer in particular often finds the shortest shots round the green the ones which cause real trouble. For this reason I usually suggest to pupils that they spend plenty of time practising extremely short chips – much smaller than one would normally face on the course. This helps produce tremendous control. If one can develop touch for these shots of just a few feet – as small as 8 or 10 feet – then the rest usually fall into place quite simply. The important point here is to shorten both backswing and through-

106. For the good golfer the important thing in chipping is feel and judgement. This is improved by using the hands and wrists, the address position now being very compact, hands ahead of the ball, elbows in.

106

swing, ultimately being able to produce a really smooth action with the clubhead just travelling a foot or so either way. This, in fact, sounds rather easier than it is. Most long handicap golfers take the club back much too far for all these shots, from there slowing up through the ball and producing a very short, loose follow-through. In slowing up, the left arm once again stops and the wrists fold up. Correctly, however short the shot, the backswing must be sufficiently small that one can hit the ball with the arms travelling at a steady pace, keeping the left one moving through impact. This produces the firm, controlled finish always seen in a good short game action, striking the ball with a really reliable, solid contact.

More advanced chipping and pitching

For the longer handicap woman golfer, the short game needs all the emphasis laid on firmness and the use of the large muscles of the arms and back. But beyond this initial stage of the pendulum swing, we become more and more concerned with acquiring a delicate touch and perfect judgement. We are no longer mainly concerned with striking the ball satisfactorily; this by now is instinctive. What we want is to start getting the ball within safe one putt distance more and more regularly, first with chipping and then ultimately with longer pitch shots. So we want 'feel' and for this we need to begin emphasizing the use of the small muscles of the hands, wrists and fingers. Perhaps this part, more than any other, is where the woman golfer should really excel.

So, for the more advanced

107. The club is taken back almost entirely with the hands, the right elbow close to the body.

108. In the throughswing the wrists remain cocked so that the back of the left wrist is straight or even arched through impact.

109. Despite the use of the hands and wrists in the backswing the followthrough is very firm, the right knee just working through to the target and the eyes 'glued' to the spot where the ball was.

107

108

109

golfer, the address position for the chip is compact, the grip well down the shaft, the hands a little ahead of the ball and, on a really short shot, the elbows relaxed into the side. A start was made in opening the stance for the beginner – just turning the toes towards the target. For the better player the line across the toes can actually point well left of target which helps one get through and also keeps the club travelling slightly longer towards the flag. The shoulders, however, stay square (Fig. 106). Quite a contrast to the stiff position necessary for the longer handicap player.

The hands in the short game

The backswing is now initiated very much with the hands, so that the wrists break very early and freely in the takeaway (Fig. 107). For the smallest shots hardly any movement in the right arm will be seen. It is all in the hands. But from here through the ball the arms begin to take over. The wrists remain cocked, for the most perfect feel almost seeming to cock slightly more in the start of the downswing, and so working through the ball with the left wrist and forearm very definitely leading the clubhead (Figs. 108 and 109).

The essential here is the soft, smooth hand action on the backswing but the firmness of the arms from there through. Very much the same applies to pitching, cocking the wrists

really early and freely, but ensuring that the left arm is firm right through the ball. It is this which is so hard for the beginner to grasp. If she uses the hands in the backswing, she invariably uncocks them fully by impact. She must aim at a stiff, reliable method. The good golfer must

work on developing feel with the hands to chip the ball consistently within one putt range. One additional tip with really short chip shots is to address the ball rather towards the toe of the club. This gives a softer contact and more delicate feel to the ball.

110

110. Looking down on the sand wedge with the face in a square position.

The cut shot

The open clubface

Although the sand wedge produces quite a high shot just through using the standard loft built into it, sometimes one needs to get the ball up especially high yet stop it very quickly once it hits the green. The ordinary loft of the sand wedge isn't sufficient. One therefore has to adapt the club and swing to produce this much higher trajectory. What we do is to 'open' the clubface, so increasing the effective loft. Firstly, one can do this just by tipping the hands back behind the ball. This increases the loft very slightly but it has its limits. If one moves the hands back more than a couple of inches it is difficult to get a good contact without catching the ground behind the ball. The second way is to keep the shaft pointing straight upwards, allowing the head to turn away to the right and at the same time increasing the loft. This must be done *before* the grip is set (Figs. 110 and 111).

The basic cut shot shot

The longer handicap player can use this open clubface position with her stiff pendulum swing, just taking a little longer swing both back and through to make up for the extra height. What one notices here is that as well as taking off with a little more height the ball tends to drift away very slightly to the right. One therefore off-sets this by aiming the stance and whole swing a little to the left. At first the easiest way of judging this is to pick a target say 2 yards left of the flag and to think of landing the ball there. In fact the ball should drift slightly to the right and so directly to the flag. The main point in first attempting this is to overcome the odd appearance of the clubhead and to remember to alter the club-

111

111. To produce greater height with the sand wedge the face can be opened before the grip is set, giving a greater effective loft but also meaning that the face is turned out to the right. In using the open face the ball drifts out to the right so that the whole stance and swing is aimed left of target to allow for this.

112

113

114

115

116

116

117

112–117. The cut shot shows a
steep wristy action in the
backswing, sliding the clubhead
beneath the ball in an open
position and so cutting it sharply
upwards.

head *before* setting the grip. In opening the clubface in this way, it is rather easy to let the ball get too near the heel of the club, so care must be taken to position it perhaps a little towards the toe.

This stiff, pendulum action with an open face is a very good safety pitch even for the top class player. In a tight situation with a tricky shot over a small bunker this is perhaps more reliable and less susceptible to pressure than any method using the hands. However, as one comes to need an even higher shot, the hands have to be brought into the action and the swing adapted. This is the true cut shot.

The idea here is that one increases the backspin on the ball, not just through increasing the loft of the club, but by actually cutting under the ball, more or less sliding the clubhead beneath it.

An advanced cut shot

The way to learn this is to start with the ball on a really good lie – perhaps with ½ inch of grass beneath it. The clubface is laid right back, almost so that the back of it seems flat on the ground. The club is then picked up rather sharply with the hands and then in the throughswing the clubface is held open and actually slid beneath the ball. In doing this, the ball pops up very steeply but drifts noticeably to the right. One therefore off-sets this by aiming the whole stance and swing left of target, in fact, in the experimental stage, picking a new target left of the flag. In technical terms this amounts to opening the stance and swinging from out-to-in. However, mention of this often makes it sound considerably more difficult than just saying one aims left and allows for the ball to drift right. The two are really just the same. If one is a sufficiently accomplished golfer to be able to think of swinging a little from out-to-in the club can, in fact, be picked up even more steeply, with even greater wristcock, and so imparting even more backspin. But this is certainly only advice for the single figure handicap player (Figs. 112–117).

With a little practice the good golfer can eventually master this shot from comparatively tight lies on the fairway – though it is always easier the thicker the cushion of grass. The best practice, I think, is to play from behind a tree, perhaps 15 to 20 feet high, cutting the ball up more and more quickly and seeing just how close one can get to the tree and still be able to get it up and over. It is surprising the height and steepness one can achieve.

This type of cut shot can then be adapted for the longer pitches to the green, perhaps of 60 or 70 yards with the pitching wedge. The stance and backswing are much the same, this time *not* sliding the clubhead under the ball, but squeezing it away with a divot. The slightly open clubface will impart a little extra backspin and produce a shot which lands softly on the green. This is the fairly standard type of long pitch shot for the better player.

The drawn pitch

When one comes to the really top class player, perhaps 4 handicap and below, great advantage is found if the ball can be worked into the green either with a slight cut or slight draw. The cut shot is usually well mastered by this time; the drawn pitch is usually ignored. Although the cut pitch lands and stops quickly there is always a danger of dropping it short. It is a rather weak shot and doesn't bore through the air. If one can draw the ball very slightly it keeps travelling against any breeze and yet will sit down well on a watered green. The secret here is the stance. The feet are now aimed to the right of target with the face of the sand wedge or pitching wedge feeling exaggeratedly closed, aimed perhaps 30° left of target. The backswing is now on the inside, attacking the ball along the line of the feet and so considerably in-to-out. The surprising thing about this is that however much one seems to shut the clubface very little hook is actually seen. The position can be really exaggerated, attacking the ball very much from the inside but with the clubface closed. The ball will then move slightly from the right to left – one can feel the difference off the clubface even if the bend is hardly noticeable – and hold its direction into the green. This is a most useful shot from 50 to 100 yards from the green and, particularly when the greens are watered and the flags at the back, far more effective than the more usual slightly cut pitch.

11 THE ART OF PUTTING

The main difficulty with teaching putting is that it is a highly individual part of the game, with very few real rights and wrongs. The variation seen in the styles of good putters bears this out. There are all sorts of stances and grips, postures and putting strokes, so that it is awfully hard to lay down a set of hard and fast rules for the perfect putting method. Obviously a great deal of the ability of the really brilliant putters is a question of having a marvellous eye for putting – being able to see the line and stroke the ball smoothly along it. Without this one is never likely to be an exceptional putter, but to become at least an average putter is largely a matter of grooving a sound stroke and having plenty of practice.

Gripping the putter

With the golf swing there are really certain types of grips one simply has to conform to in order to be successful. In putting, there is no definite right and wrong way to grip the club – except, of course, whether or not it works. One can use the ordinary golf grip, a split handed grip in which the hands are separated, or even a cack-handed grip in which the left is below the right, or, in fact, anything which gives results.

Perhaps the commonest grip amongst good putters is the reverse overlap grip, which is basically the ordinary Vardon grip, but with the index finger of the left hand down the outside of the fingers of the right, or round the knuckle of the index finger of the right (Fig. 118). For the player without a good grip and method of putting this is perhaps the one to adopt. It has the advantage over the ordinary grip of setting the left hand in a position where it can push the club back on the line with rather more authority. In the ordinary grip the left hand is predominantly on top of the club, the right hand below.

With putting, the palms should be directly to the sides of the club, thumbs right on top of the shaft. For this reason the putter grip is usually flat on top, not rounded like the rest of the set.

118

The stance

Putting stances of top class professionals show every kind of extreme. There are those players who position the ball opposite the left heel and others with it far nearer the right. Some adopt an open stance, others a closed one. Some stand very tall to the ball, while others crouch right over, gripping halfway down the shaft. It is all largely a question of comfort, confidence and control.

The most conventional stance

118. One of the most popular grips for putting is the reverse overlap grip in which the left index finger rides down the outside of the fingers of the right hand.

119. An address position for putting, the ball just inside the left heel, arms close to the body.

for the beginner to copy is to position the ball just inside the left foot, feet comfortably apart with the weight favouring the left foot. The hands should be level with or slightly ahead of the clubhead, clubface square, and with the right elbow fairly close to the body (Fig. 119). Whether one prefers to crouch down low or stand very upright is largely a matter of eyesight. Crouching low perhaps gives one a closer look at the line and more control of the putter; standing up to the putt gives one a better view of the whole area between the ball and the hole for a longer one.

A common error in the stance is to let the hands drop too low and to bring them too close to the legs. Not only does this tend to raise the toe off the ground, instead of having the sole of the putter flat on it, but it restricts the hands in the backswing and means that the putter cannot move straight back from the ball. Correctly then, the putter is flat on the ground with the hands just clear of the legs (Fig. 120). Here we see the one really definite rule of putting. The eyes are directly above the ball, making it as easy as possible to judge the line to the hole. If the eyes are ever outside the ball the tendency is to pull it to the left; on the other hand if they are very much inside the ball the putt is likely to be pushed to the right. In practice to have the eyes slightly inside the ball can give some players a clearer view of the line than to have them directly above it. This is largely, one assumes, a matter of eyesight. What one must never do, however, is to let them move outside the ball. This is a sure sign of trouble.

The stroke

As the putter is taken back it should move straight along the line of the putt, with the club close to the ground (Fig. 121). Only on a really long putt does it need to start coming inside this line. From here the putter must accelerate through to the hole, the eyes still looking at the spot where the ball was until it is well on its way (Fig. 122). It is largely this steady head position which controls the throughswing. If the eyes move too soon, the head moves, the shoulders in turn move, and the putter is almost certain to come off-line to either right or left. Particularly on a short putt learn to keep the head anchored and *hear* the ball drop in. Don't see it drop.

120. In the basic putting stroke the eyes are directly over the ball making it as easy as possible to judge the straight line from the ball to the hole.

121. The putter moves back on a straight line, low to the ground and still square to the hole.

122. In the action through the ball the putter head stays close to the ground, following through towards the hole on the same straight line. The eyes are still glued on the spot where the ball was, keeping the shoulders from moving and so taking the putter off-line.

120

121

Practising the stroke

One of the best ways of learning a good stroke is to practise swinging the club along a line, either along a clubshaft or, better still, between two clubs. This trains one to keep the club moving straight back and through, making any inconsistency quite obvious. A second way is to practise pushing the ball to the hole, without any backswing. This type of push stroke is illegal on the course, but as a practice technique it teaches one to keep the clubhead moving on target beyond the ball. It also stresses the idea of accelerating to the hole. Most of us, tournament professional and club golfer alike, are guilty of taking too long a backswing, then slowing up through impact.

By learning to roll the putt with this push stroke, or practising with a really short backswing, emphasis is put on the action *through* to the hole. Again, just as in the long game and rest of the short game, holding a really firm finish is a check-point for what has gone before.

Another excellent way of training the putting stroke is to swing back and through and then on every putt to return the clubhead to the address position. This does two important things. Firstly, it helps one to see any discrepancy in the stroke; it is very obvious if one has to steer the club back to address. Secondly, it makes one conscious of bringing the putter back and so helps one not to look up too soon. The shoulders move in a consistent path, bringing the putter back and through on line.

Reading the greens

As well as developing a good, repetitive putting stroke, the newer golfer needs to learn how to read the greens, judging both the speed of the ball and the amount of break from one side or the other. Once you know the kind of thing to look for, reading the greens is largely a matter of experience, both with your home course and unfamiliar ones.

Judging speed

Let's deal first with the speed of the putt. The first thing to look at, of course, is whether you are putting uphill or downhill. Very often this is quite obvious. If it isn't then one can look at the putt from the side to get a better idea of the fall of the ground. Secondly, the texture and dampness of the ground is important. Where the grass is very short and dry and the ground hard, the ball will roll much more quickly than it will on rather thicker, damper grass. This naturally changes both during the day and from day to day. When the greens have just been cut the ball will run faster; by contrast, early in the morning and late in the evening they tend to be moist – the moisture rising up through the ground – and this makes the putt considerably slower.

As you get to know your home course rather better, you will probably begin to find a pattern of inconsistency amongst the greens, with some always putting much slower or more quickly than others. A well elevated, plateau green, for example, will often drain very quickly, becoming much faster than the rest, and certainly much faster than one which lies in a basin and so gathers moisture. A very open green, exposed to both sun and wind, tends to dry out quickly, where a green built very much amongst trees tends to hold moisture, getting less than its fair share of sun. After a while, one begins to recognize inconsistencies on unfamiliar greens very easily, spotting these kinds of features the first time one plays them.

Speed and grain

Lastly there is the 'grain' of the green, not a problem in Great Britain, but one which affects golfers in many other countries. The grass has a definite way of growing, either with the rising and setting of the sun, towards water, away from mountains, or just in the way most people walk across the green. If the grass is growing towards you it will look dark and matt; if it is growing away from you then it appears much lighter and shinier – much the same as the two-tone effect of a newly-cut green. The ball will run considerably more with the grain, or, in other words, with the growth of the grass, and will pull up quickly into the grain.

These, then, are the kinds of things to look for in judging speed. The basic ones, of course, are the slope and the thickness of the grass, but the other points gradually begin to make sense as one plays on more and more courses and different types of greens.

Judging the borrow

In judging the 'borrow' – the amount one needs to allow from the side – the main point is once more the slope of the ground. To examine this, crouch down behind the ball, trying to get a good overall idea of the lie of the land, but paying most attention to the part right around the hole. The ball is travelling at its slowest here so that this is where the break really begins to have effect. Very often the slope of the ground is quite obvious, but if it isn't, one can often get some help by looking at the whole contour of the green and even the fairway or ground surrounding it. If the whole of this breaks a certain way, the chances are your putt will do just the same. Where the green is obviously at a different angle from the fairway, the contours can be quite confusing. In this case it is a good idea to try to find something to use as a reference to the vertical, either picking out a tree or building in the background, by hanging the putter at arm's length in front of you or even by replacing the flag in the centre of the hole while you line up the putt.

Lastly, on greens which show a definite grain, one has to have a clear picture of this. If one is putting across the grain this often has much more effect on the line of the putt than any slope. The putt may be perfectly flat but the grain will take it off to one side or the other, in the direction of the growth of the grass.

123

124

125

Long putts

The essence of good long putting is judging the distance well. Except on a tremendously sloping green one is unlikely to be very far out on direction, but with a really long putt it is quite possible to be a matter of yards out on the distance. So one wants a method which gives a nice, sensitive feel. Just as with chipping, if one can bring the hands and fingers into use here, rather than just employing the large, less sensitive muscles of the arms and shoulders, it is simpler to develop better touch and judgement. Standing up well with a long putt usually gives the player the best possible view of the line, from here taking the club back with a smooth, soft action of the hands and arms, but swinging through with a predominantly arm action (Figs. 123–125). In judging the

123–125. For a longer putt the hands and wrists can be brought into the action, giving an improved feel for distance.

126. With a long putt on a fast green one can judge the whole curve of the putt and just send the ball off along this (dotted line). With a slower green one can pick out a spot to the side of the hole and think of banging the ball firmly to this (solid line).

FAST

SLOW

126

127

128

129

exact distance, have several practice swings in which you actually look at the hole to try to 'feel' the strength of the putt. Having decided how much the ball will break, either try to see the whole curve of the putt – particularly where it is fast and there is considerable borrow – and just concentrate on sending the ball off along this; or on a slower, straighter putt where you are striking the ball much harder, pick out a spot to the appropriate side of the hole and purely concentrate on banging the ball at that (Fig. 126).

Short putts

With short putts, particularly when the green is not unduly fast, the main concern is the direction rather than the speed. Here one is unlikely to overshoot the hole by very far and the exact line becomes the main aim. For these types of putts, a better method, particularly for the club golfer, shows a rather stiffer, more controlled action. This relies very much more on the use of the arms and shoulders and cutting out hand action. In this case the wrists and arms are much stiffer at address, taking the club back with a pendulum movement from the shoulders and no hinging of the wrists, from here pushing the putter through once more with the arms (Figs. 127–129). Notice in the followthrough that the head is absolutely steady – the number one rule for short putting.

When the greens are comparatively slow, one can usually pick a spot to the side of the hole, or at the lip of the hole, striking the ball firmly at this. One is far more concerned with getting this direction than worrying too exactly about speed. As the green gets faster, however, one has to start judging speed

127–129. The most reliable method of short putting for the club player is a predominantly stiff action from the arms and shoulders, with no breaking of the wrists in either backswing or throughswing.

130. With a short, sidehill putt one can either hit the ball firmly for the hole (solid line), the main danger being that a missed putt will run several feet past, or one can stroke it much more gently, but allowing for a much bigger break (dotted line) which is rather harder to judge accurately.

DIFFICULT TO JUDGE

DANGEROUS

and borrow together (Fig. 130). Let's look at a fast 5 or 6-foot putt with a definite break from right to left. One can tackle this in several ways. At one extreme one can really bang the ball straight for the hole. Because it is travelling quite fast it takes up little break. But if it does miss it is likely to run 8 or 10-feet past. Then at the other end of the scale, one can let the ball travel very, very slowly so that it dies into the front side of the hole. This is safer in that one is certain to leave it within a matter of inches, but it is terribly hard to judge exactly. The ball may well break a foot or more. Ideally, then, one chooses something in between the two, settling on a speed which would only run the ball past 18 inches to 2 feet and also cutting down slightly on the borrow.

Ball position and sidehill lies

For these types of sidehill putts the position of the feet can be altered slightly to help keep the ball up on the higher side of the hole. The theory here is that it is much better to over-borrow than under-borrow. A ball which is above the hole always has the chance of turning and rolling into it; once it is below the hole it can never drop. With a putt which breaks from right to left one wants, therefore, to keep the ball up to the right if anything. To help do this the ball can be played further back in the stance, in other words more towards the right foot. With a putt which breaks from the left the ball is best played a little further to the left in the stance, if anything making one more likely to pull it to the left and so keep it up on the high side of the hole.

Choosing a putter

Four main kinds

Putting is very largely a matter of confidence, so that it is important to feel really happy with the putter you choose. There are really four main classes, all of which have their merits and failings. The first is the old-fashioned blade putter – very similar in design to the long irons, except, of course, that the loft is virtually nil. These clubs are often used tremendously well, but on the other hand they perhaps exaggerate any fault in the putting stroke. Every club has a 'sweet spot' – the part giving the most solid contact with the ball – and in the blade putter this spot is often very small. If one doesn't quite strike it bang in the middle, the club tends to twist and the ball can easily be sent off-line (Fig. 131).

The second type of putter is the mallet putter – very similar to the blade putter but with a flange built out at the back of the club. This has the same type of problem as the blade putter in respect of the sweet spot, but because of the piece built out at the back, it often means that the manufacturer includes a line to give you a good guide to the sweet spot, and this also helps one judge whether the club is swung through smoothly on line. This then gives some advantage over the ordinary blade.

The third type of putter sets about eliminating the twisting action of the club when the ball is struck slightly off-centre. Instead of having the shaft angled into the head at the heel, it is joined very much nearer the centre of the head – hence the name 'centre-shafted putter'. Now the sweet spot is much nearer the shaft and any tendency to hit the ball slightly away from this results in much less twist to the head.

The fourth main kind aims at doing much the same thing – this time actually expanding the sweet spot of the club. This is done by weighting the club very much at the heel and toe and so giving a wider space at the centre of the club to hit the ball solidly. This kind of 'heel-toe' putter again minimizes the fault of the club golfer who strikes the ball off-centre. These putters, however, often look bulky and perhaps don't inspire the confidence they should for the newer golfer.

The main point about choosing a putter is to be happy with it. For the newer golfer a standard centre-shafted putter is perhaps the safest buy, looking also for a slight 'wry' in the neck. This is a little kink which sets the shaft ahead of the face, in turn setting the hands a little ahead of the ball – always a good thing in putting. But again, whether one chooses a wry-necked putter or not is a matter of personal preference and confidence.

The lie

What does matter in choosing a putter is the lie of the club. This refers to the angle at which the shaft comes out of the head. If the shaft comes up almost vertically the putter is described as being 'upright', encouraging the player to hold the hands high above the ball. When the shaft comes out from the head at far

131

131. The four basic types of putter. From left to right, the blade, the mallet, the centre-shafted putter and the heel-toe putter

more of an angle, this is known as a flat lie. This is more suitable to the player who holds the hands low and close to the body. The danger here is that the hands can get too close to the legs, inhibiting the backswing. The point is that the sole of the club must sit flat on the ground when you feel to be in a comfortable position. Until one is set in a particular style, a more upright putter is generally a better choice, encouraging one to keep the hands high and the eyes above the ball.

Length and weight

As for both weight and length, my own feeling is that many putters are both too heavy and too long for women. The longer and heavier the putter the more delicate the swing has to be. By contrast, if one uses a lighter club with a shorter shaft it is possible to take a little more swing for the same length of putt. Particularly as most golfers are guilty of taking too much backswing this helps minimize the fault. This factor, however, is very dependent on the type of greens on which one plays. Lush, grassy greens which tend to be slow are often more suited to a heavy putter; fast bare greens require a lighter touch and in turn a lighter putter. Personally I feel it is a good thing to have more than one putter – many professionals have literally dozens. One can then change the club with a change of greens and also discard anything which falls out of favour. A change of putter, a change of stance or even a change of grip is one of the best ways of beating lack of confidence on the greens, and confidence – particularly with the putter – is one of the vital things to the golfer.

12 TAKING THE FEAR OUT OF BUNKERS

Buying your way out of bunkers

The first essential of good bunker play is to have a good sand wedge; without one, no amount of teaching is going to do much good.

The sand wedge is like the putter and driver. To the tournament professional they are perhaps the most important clubs in the bag. He or she may change the rest of the irons and woods fairly frequently but these clubs are kept from year to year. Of the three, it is often the sand wedge which is the most valued.

There are good manufacturers who design terrible wedges and there are less good manufacturers who hit on a successful design. The majority of professionals, however, seem to choose much the same thing – a club with a nicely curved leading edge (the line along the bot-

132

132. Incorrect. The typical action of the longer handicap player shows an attempt to scoop the ball out, falling back onto the right foot and either thinning it into the bank or taking too much sand.

tom of the face), a medium flange (the broader sole of the

sand wedge) and with the front of the club not unduly raised off the ground. Let's look at my own club. The leading edge is nicely rounded so that as I turn the clubhead into an open position for added height the leading edge hardly seems to have moved away from the line (Figs. 110 and 111). If the leading edge is straight, immediately the face is opened the whole club seems to turn away from the shot, so that the club certainly appears more difficult to use.

In choosing a sand wedge ask the advice of your professional. Don't necessarily take the one that matches the rest of your set but be prepared to browse through even the most ancient of secondhand clubs to find what you want. Having found one which suits you hang onto it even when you do buy a new set. A good sand wedge is the one club you really can't do without.

Splashing from a bunker

The basic bunker shot never need be treated with fear. Once one can get the right idea of it, the actual swing is physically very easy. Most players panic in a bunker; the majority have never had a lesson on bunker shots so that their natural instincts are all wrong. The usual fault is to try to lift or scoop the ball out, falling back onto the right foot in an attempt to get under the ball. All this does is to catch the ball very thin, scuttling it into the bank, or to catch the sand way behind it with a chopping action (Fig. 132).

Think of the sand forget the ball

It is the right picture which is so important. The main thing to realize in any bunker shot from around the green is that the sand is very much more important than the ball. If one can splash out a handful of sand with the ball in the middle of it, the ball will pop out too. In playing a bunker shot one has to visualize this handful of sand around the ball, purely concentrating on this and letting the ball be completely incidental. The first stage in learning this 'splash shot'

should be without the ball, picking the sand wedge up very steeply and swinging down and through the sand, splashing away a few inches of it. This is really terribly easy. The next stage is to try to judge where you are going to take this handful. In your first attempts some of the splashes are likely to come opposite your left foot and some opposite your right. Now we have to get them all in much the same place. This time draw a line in the sand, perhaps 6 feet long, and stand astride one end of this, facing down the line. Now practise swinging and splashing through the sand, each time brushing away part of the line with a full, free but fairly slow swing. In doing this pick the club up quite quickly in the backswing, making sure that you are onto the left foot by the end of the followthrough. Once you can do this quite easily, brushing away the line, you can move on to doing the same thing with the ball.

Learning the shot

My first stage with teaching bunker shots with the ball is to draw an oval mark around it in the sand, from 2½ inches behind the ball to 2½ inches beyond it. This helps the pupil to concentrate on splashing out

133–138. The idea in the bunker shot is to splash out a handful of sand with the ball in the middle of it. Weight is kept on the left foot throughout, picking the club up sharply in the backswing and then swinging through the sand very smoothly to a full followthrough.

the sand and not the ball. The ball is then positioned perhaps a third of the way from left foot to right foot, feet slightly shuffled in for a firm stance and the weight favouring the left foot. The clubhead should be held as close to the sand as possible without touching it, *not* right behind the ball but just above the back of the oval mark. This is the point you want to enter the sand, so your club is positioned over this point with the eyes firmly focused on it (Fig. 133).

The swing

From here the club should be picked up steeply, using plenty of wristcock, to a fairly full swing. Two points are particularly important here. Firstly the eyes must be kept on the spot in the sand and secondly the weight should stay central in the feet or still slightly on the left. This encourages the correct downward attack into the ball (Fig. 134).

In approaching impact there are four main points on which to concentrate. Firstly, the eyes must always stay focused on the same spot in the sand, never shifting to the ball. Secondly, the weight must never fall back onto the right foot but must stay on the left in the throughswing. Thirdly, one must not attack the shot with too much force. The clubhead will penetrate the sand more easily with the club travelling at a fairly slow, constant speed. If one rushes at the ball, the sand builds up tremendous resistance to the clubhead and it is difficult to move it on through. So the swing must be unrushed. Lastly, the club not only has to enter the sand in the right place but it has to come on through and out of the sand the other side. The idea, let's remember, is to splash out the handful of sand, *not* just to dig in the sand behind the ball. The club is therefore swung very smoothly from the top of the backswing, splashing out the handful of

133

134

135

sand, swinging through to a really full, balanced follow-through (Figs. 135–138).

Four main rules

These, then, are the four rules for the basic splash shot. Think only of the handful of sand you want to take, *not* the ball. If the sand comes out so will the ball. Secondly, keep the weight favouring the left foot for a steep, downward attack. Thirdly, swing smoothly and slowly to penetrate the sand better and fourthly, remember to go through the sand and out the other side, to a really full follow-through.

At first I don't worry too much about the angle of the clubface – this can often confuse the newer golfer – but ideally it should be quite open, increasing the effective loft but aiming away to the right (Figs. 110 and 111). With experience with the shot one gradually finds that this tends to make the ball drift away to the right, so that one actually aims and swings rather to the left of the target, in other words, using a slightly open stance and swinging a little from 'out-to-in.' These are finer points of technique, however, and need not concern the beginner immediately (Figs. 139–143).

The main danger for the woman golfer is of quitting in the sand, losing speed by impact, or of trying to flick the clubhead through with the hands and wrists. Unlike with the long shots, one doesn't want any speedy hand action through the ball. Although the wrists are active in the backswing, producing this high, steep swing, the uncocking action must come very gradually and largely beyond impact. The idea I like to use with the pupil who finds it difficult not to flick at the ball with the hands, is of swinging a very, very heavy club or even something like a sledge hammer. The feeling is then one of having to swing really slowly, with a kind of tension in the arms and wrists which does not let the hands flick on through. The swing can then become much more deliberate, with a constant speed throughout the downswing, not a sudden flick of the clubhead at the ball.

Judging distance

Judging distance with the splash shot is a combination of three factors. Firstly, one can vary the amount of sand taken. The smaller the splash of sand the less the blow on the ball is cushioned and so the further the ball travels. If one takes a larger, deeper splash of sand, the ball will travel a shorter distance. Secondly, one can vary the speed of the swing and the length of the swing, shortening it and slowing it down very slightly for a shorter shot. Thirdly, one can gradually open the clubface a little more, keeping the swing constant, to produce a shorter, higher shot. The pro-

136

137

138

139

140

140

139–143. To produce plenty of height from the bunker the clubface is opened, giving it more loft but also meaning that it turns out to the right. To off-set this the whole set-up and swing is aimed a few feet left of target, the ball now popping up quickly and still travelling on target.

141

142

143

144

145

146

144–146. With the ball buried in the sand the clubface is set square or even slightly closed, picking it up sharply in the backswing and really smashing down into the back of it with as much force as possible.

fessional instinctively uses a combination of all three of these, relying on experience for this judgement. For the newer golfer, varying the amount of sand taken and the angle of the clubface are much easier alterations than actually changing the swing. If the beginner tries to slow down the swing or change its length, she usually loses the original idea of the shot. So keep the swing the same, taking more sand or opening the clubface wider for a shorter shot, and taking less sand or squaring up the clubface for a longer one.

Playing from heavy sand and hard sand

Many bunkers are not really filled with sand, but with a type of heavy shingle. The difficulty here is that it resists the clubhead; the deeper one goes into it the greater the resistance. Speed is then very easily lost and distance hard to control. The first point is to take care with the stance, trying not to let the feet sink too deep. If they do, the bottom of the swing is likely to be well below the ball. To produce a shallower contact with the ball, the backswing needs to be wider, taking the club back low and without the distinct lift needed in the ordinary shot, but taking care not to touch the sand in the takeaway. The attack on the ball is now much shallower, skimming the top layer of sand on which the ball sits, so that resistance is kept to a minimum. The margins here are slightly finer than with the ordinary shot, meaning that one has to judge the depth exactly, but once mastered, it is a much safer way of tackling heavy sand. Distance can then be varied by progressively opening the clubface.

When the sand is very shallow with a hard surface beneath, one needs much the same kind of approach, avoiding going too deep. The added problem here is that the flange on the back of the sand wedge tends to catch this hard layer, bouncing upwards and striking the ball thinly. In this case, instead of opening the clubface, it is held square, hands slightly ahead of it, which keeps the front edge of the club low and if anything raises the flange slightly. If there is a reasonable amount of sand, the shot can then be played in much the same way as the ordinary splash shot, taking care to keep the swing smooth and slow, and with a slightly shallower takeaway and attack as from heavy sand. When the ground becomes really bare and hard, the swing can be cut down, using very little hand action and playing the shot like a stiff-wristed pitch shot, with a smooth, deliberate action through the ball, taking it off as cleanly as possible.

148. With a short shot from an uphill lie the easiest shot is often to chip it out, taking the ball first and then going through the sand beyond.

Exploding from a buried lie

The basic bunker shot is, or should be, comparatively easy. But particularly when one isn't playing in tournament conditions the lies in bunkers aren't always good like the ones one first learns from. The basic splash shot then needs adapting to get out safely. As the lie gets worse one needs to concentrate on going slightly lower beneath the ball, splashing out a slightly deeper scoop of sand. The weight has to favour the left foot even more and one has to shuffle in the feet a little deeper. But when the ball actually gets buried or partly buried, one has to change the approach altogether.

With this buried lie, the sand wedge should never be opened; if it is, the face tends to be opened even more as it meets the sand. In this case the club should be set to the ball with the face square or even fractionally closed – slightly left-aimed with the loft diminished – and the hands well ahead of the clubhead. The ball is positioned rather further back in the feet, around the middle of the stance, with the weight once more on the left foot and the feet shuffled in for a firm base (Fig. 144). The

147

147. With the ball sitting well on an uphill lie the body is set back, shoulders parallel to the slope so that the swing can travel up the slope and not into it. The handful of sand is taken as usual, concentrating on swinging through to a full finish.

eyes are focused just behind the ball – again not actually on it – and the backswing is steep with a distinct lift to it (Fig. 145). The downswing is now an almost chopping action with as much force as one can summon up (Fig. 146). Playing out of a buried lie like this really is just strength. So give yourself maximum chance of getting out; aim to the closest point clear of the bunker which seems practical, not necessarily to the flag, and concentrate on smashing right down into the sand just behind the ball.

Uphill and downhill shots

Uphill

One of the more difficult types of bunker shots is the splash shot from an uphill lie. It looks easy enough, but the problem is that one is likely to strike the ball before the sand instead of taking sand all round the ball. The attack must no longer be a steep downward one, but must be a slightly shallower one, travelling upwards in striking the sand to follow the line of the slope. The weight must therefore be pushed back onto the right foot so that the body is roughly at right angles to the slope, the shoulders following it. The shot is now executed much the same as from the flat lie, entering the sand behind the ball and sweeping on through it to a full finish (Fig. 147). As the slope gets steeper, so the weight has to fall more and more onto the right foot, taking a fuller swing and allowing for the ball to go off with greater and greater height.

A short shot from a slightly uphill lie, particularly where the bank is low, really lends itself to being chipped out. The weight can then be kept slightly on the left foot, this time hitting the ball and then the sand, taking a short

149–151. On a downhill lie or from a hole in the bunker, the weight is kept exaggeratedly on the left foot, right shoulder very high. The club is then picked up steeply, even letting the left arm bend slightly, to produce a really steep downward attack in which the club continues to travel on down beyond the ball.

149

150

151

swing and punching it away firmly (Fig. 148).

Downhill

The main problem as always with a downhill lie is to avoid hitting the ground, or, in this case, the sand behind the ball. Not only is this the main factor in the downswing but it is also vital in the backswing, being a breach of rules, of course, if one brushes the sand. The weight is therefore set really exaggeratedly on the left foot, in turn raising the right shoulder and immediately setting one up for a steeper backswing (Fig. 149). The club must then be picked up really sharply with the hands, and even letting the left arm break slightly at the elbow to make this more pronounced (Fig. 150). The weight is then kept well on the left foot, following down the line of the ground through impact (Fig. 151) and taking the club on through to a full, controlled finish. Exactly this same technique can be used in playing out of a deep hole or footprint, picking the club up as quickly as possible and chopping steeply down and through the sand.

Long bunker shots

In playing a long bunker shot the lie is very important in determining the kind of shot one plays. If the lie is less than perfect, with the ball sitting at all below the surface, it has to be punched out, taking the ball first followed by the sand. This is really the equivalent of striking the ball with a divot. The ball can then be positioned roughly opposite the centre of the stance, keeping the weight if anything favouring the left foot, and then hitting down and through the ball. In this case the eyes are fixed on the back of the ball just as with the standard fairway shot. As far as clubbing goes, the main point is to get out. Don't gamble too much, but have a good look at the shot from the side to assess how much height is needed to clear the lip. If there is any doubt take the more lofted club but otherwise allow one more club than from the fairway. With this type of lie the medium and long irons are not always easy for the longer handicap player because, as from grass, they need quite a degree of strength to be punched out in this way. With the short irons this type of contact produces a good, crisp shot, and is ideal for playing 50, 60 or 70-yard pitch shots from the sand, shortening the swing and punching the ball away.

When the lie is perfect and the ball sits right on top of the sand, it can be swept away absolutely cleanly. Providing there is no lip to catch the ball this type of contact is quite possible even with the long irons. In this case the feet are not shuffled in and the swing is wide and high, concentrating on picking the ball off without any sand. An adjustment which makes this easier is to look, not at the back of the ball, but more towards the top of it, making one all the more likely to hit the ball cleanly. In this case the ball usually travels virtually the same distance as from the fairway, if anything, perhaps, a little further. The main point here is a good, clean contact without taking any sand at all.

13 OTHER SHOTS FOR BETTER SCORING

Length from a poor lie

Usually I suppose when most golfers practise, they give themselves good or at least average lies; this is fine for it builds up confidence and lets one develop a repeatable swing. But in transferring this learning to the course the lies aren't always quite so perfect and the problems become rather different. The woman golfer is always somewhat hampered by a poor lie on the fairway; having less strength in the wrists really begins to show in this situation. She is far less able to get herself out of trouble simply through using brute force.

Let's look at the fairway shot from a tight lie or shallow divot hole. Unless the woman golfer is a really good one, the long irons simply don't lend themselves to this situation. The longer blade often doesn't fit any depression or set itself so easily to the bottom of the ball. Added to this, it needs a really strong swing and grip to keep the club moving through both ball and turf from this type of lie.

Instead of using the 3-iron, a very much better choice is the 5-wood, or failing this a 4-wood. The small, chunky head of the 5-wood looks cut out for the job,

152

fitting into any divot hole far more easily than the long blade of an iron. There is also plenty of loft to get the ball up in the air. The shot can then be played in much the same way as the medium irons, positioning the ball to be caught very slightly on the downswing, taking the ball first and then a little bit of turf beyond it. The address position therefore sees the ball fairly central in the feet, with the hands slightly ahead of the ball.

One good trick here is to tip the clubhead forward – 'hooding' it so that the back of the club is raised off the

152. If the head of the 4- or 5-wood is hooded or tipped forwards slightly, it brings the back of the club off the ground and makes it easier to hit from a poor lie.

ground very slightly (Fig. 152). This gets the back of the sole out of the way and means that the clubhead can penetrate the turf without the sole plate slipping or skidding on the ground. This is especially valuable when the grass is either dry or shiny or a little wet and slippery. So keep the hands forward, clubface square or slightly hooded, hit down and through the ball and mainly have confidence in yourself and the club.

An iron shot from the tee

To make iron shots on par threes just as easy as possible, one wants to use the same type of swing as with the fairway shots. For this reason it is a mistake to tee the ball too high. To catch the ball solidly would require quite a different swing; if the swing remained the same as usual the ball would be caught from the top part of the blade, producing a rather powerless shot. Instead, push the tee well into the ground, so that the ball is just clear of the turf. All one really wants is to give the equivalent of a good lie. The ball can then be struck in just the same way as the fairway shots. The really good golfer can punch them all away with a divot while the longer handicap player can punch the short irons but sweep the ball away with the longer irons.

Playing from a steep uphill bank

In playing from a steep uphill bank, either with a full shot or around the green, one has to use much the same method as with the longer clubs from an uphill lie. If one purely hits into the bank the ball is likely to pop straight up and almost fall back to your feet. Once again one must stand so that the whole swing can follow the line of the bank, leaning back on the right foot, shoulders parallel to the hill. The takeaway now takes the club downwards to start with, from here, swinging up the slope to sweep the ball away (Fig. 153).

With a full shot the length one can get is very limited. The ball must always take off at an angle even steeper than the bank so that as one uses a longer and longer club, all that happens is that the ball goes further and further into the air without really travelling any further forwards. Something like a 7- or 8-iron is probably the easiest here – the wedge hitting the ball almost vertically and the longer irons perhaps having too long a shaft to make them really manageable.

With this type of shot from around the green, the 8- or 9-iron is probably the club, the main difficulty here being to realize just how hard one can afford to hit the ball. Most of the strength is taken up with producing height not length. Much the same type of shot can then be used from this type of lie in a bunker or from the face of a bunker, providing, of course, that the lie is good. So really lean away from the bank, shoulders following the line of the ground and concentrate on swinging the club down and then up the bank.

Driving low into the wind

There are several ways of hitting the drive lower into the wind. The first is to tee the ball down slightly, from there executing the shot in much the same way as usual. This is a good, easy way and quite sufficient for many players. However, if one is at all prone to skying the ball, teeing it lower tends to make one even more likely to chop down onto the ball – the basic fault of the skied drive – only leading to more height.

Secondly, one can play the ball fractionally further back in the feet, the idea here being that this slightly reduces the effective loft of the club. Once more the problem arises as it does with lowering the tee. Anyone

who tends to chop down onto the ball from a rather high, up-right swing is even more susceptible to doing this, only leading to increased backspin and worse height.

Thirdly, particularly for the golfer who tends to hit the ball rather high, one can aim at reducing the backspin on the ball. To do this, tee the ball an ordinary height but simply concentrate on picking it cleanly off the top of the tee, leaving it in the ground. This really only requires a slightly different mental idea of the shot – fairly simple for the experienced golfer. What it really means is that one perhaps only catches the top

9/10 of the ball, reducing the backspin and producing a shot which travels well under the wind.

153. In playing from a really steep uphill bank the body is tipped back to bring the shoulders parallel with the slope so that the followthrough can go right on up the bank.

Fairway shots in the wind

The main rule about playing fairway shots into the wind is not to fight against it. The tendency is to try to force the ball, leaning into it, chopping down on it and

producing more backspin and a higher shot than usual. Instead take plenty of club and if anything take things a little more easily than usual, keeping a

153

good, steady pace to the swing but working to a really firm, balanced finish. There are several ways of producing a lower shot. Firstly and very simply, one can use one more club than normal, the 4 instead of the 5, gripping down the club 1 inch or so to produce the length of the shorter club but with the trajectory of the longer one. Secondly one can lessen the wristcock in the backswing, producing a rather wooden swing which minimizes the backspin put on the ball. Thirdly to produce really low, punched shots the ball can be played well back in the feet, hands ahead of the ball, which reduces the effective loft of the club. The tendency here is often to push the ball to the right so that the stance has to be aimed to the left to punch the ball on target. The main thing is to be bold, take plenty of club and not to fight the wind.

As far as a crosswind goes, one has to decide whether to let the wind take the ball or whether to try to hold it into the wind – in other words, fading it into a right to left wind and drawing it into a left to right wind. Of course this is only a choice the good golfer has to make and by far the simpler way is to aim off to the side and let the wind bring the ball back. The main thing here is to judge the wind correctly. Always be on the lookout for trees down the side of a hole which protect part of the fairway or tee but leave the rest exposed. One can often stand on a tee which is surrounded by trees and not feel any breeze, while up on the green the wind is howling across it. So always try to have a good picture of what is going to happen to the ball as it reaches maximum height and when it is landing; this is where the wind has most effect. Having judged the wind, simply aim to the appropriate side, swing smoothly and really work once more to a full, controlled finish.

Playing from really thick rough

This is where women golfers really are at a disadvantage to men. We simply haven't got the strength to recover well from the rough. The top class woman golfer can keep up to a certain extent with a good man from the tee, but playing from the rough a man can drill the ball out with a 2- or 3-iron, where the poor woman is having to hack out with a wedge or 9-iron. It is just something we have to face. However, there is no need to give in altogether. The shot does require strength but it also needs the right type of approach. Most women just aren't aggressive enough from the rough. One really does have to hit the ball with brute force and a firm grip. Don't expect it to go without this. Choose a suitably short route back to the fairway, refraining from being too ambitious, choose the wedge, which is a nice, heavy weapon and then, with the weight on the left foot, pick the club up really steeply and slam it *down* into the back of the ball. Don't try to lift it. Hit really well down through the ball and it can't help but rise.

Hit down, stay down and, perhaps, calm down are the key points in recovering from the rough.

154. The 8th at Worplesdon. The best way of tackling this type of shot when the flag is on the upper layer is to run the ball in so that it rolls on up the bank. Pitching to the top layer is decidedly dangerous.

154

Playing to a two-tier green

In tournaments a course can be made much more difficult than normal by positioning the flags in strategic positions on the greens. A hole with a two-tier green can often be made far harder by putting the flag back onto the higher level. Not only does it require a longer shot, but even with a shortish pitch it requires a more finely judged shot. Very often the upper layer of the green is comparatively small, so that if one tries to pitch onto this the ball either tends to catch the bank and fall short or hit on the top and jump over. The secret here is to hit a shot so that the ball is always running as it reaches the bank between the tiers. This is by far the safest shot for the top layer (Fig. 154).

Instead of using the wedge to pitch to the green, either run the ball all the way with a 7-iron, using an extension of the chipping action, or hit a low pitch to the front of the green with an 8-iron, keeping the hands well ahead of the clubface, so that it has enough impetus to run on up the bank. For the more advanced golfer one can even produce a rather more satisfactory shot than the ordinary full 8- or 9-iron from the appropriate length, going down the shaft on a 6-iron to give a lower trajectory for much the same effect. Where the greens are particularly wet and so hold any shot, one really does have to throw caution to the wind and pitch to the top layer. But otherwise any shot which is running as it approaches the upper level is a much safer one to play.

158. One doesn't actually have to stand sideways to the hole to be able to hit the ball in the right type of direction. In an awkward position always be prepared to improvise a shot so that the club can still move back and through to the target.

Pitching from a downhill bank

One of the most difficult little shots around the green is where one has to play the ball up and over a small bunker or bank but from a position where the ball is on a severe downhill slope. One wants to get the ball up quickly but the lie makes this terribly difficult. Even the loft of the sand wedge is reduced to such an extent that the ball only seems to shoot forwards, not up. Usually the ball only settles on this type of lie if the bank is fairly grassy so that one can often play a kind of cut shot to get it up rather more quickly. As always with the downhill lie the danger is of catching the ground behind the ball. It is therefore played right opposite the right foot, leaning most exaggeratedly on the left foot so that the right shoulder is very high. The clubface is then laid back as much as possible. Opening the face in this way tends to send the ball drifting away to the right so that the whole action is aimed a few feet left of target (Fig. 155). The

155–157. The downhill pitch shot is played with a very open faced sand wedge, setting the shoulders parallel to the slope, picking the club up sharply and then following through right on down the bank beyond the ball.

155

156

157

essence of the backswing is to pick the club up really sharply with the hands, producing as steep a little backswing as possible (Fig. 156). The hands are then kept cocked as long as possible, feeling that they lead the clubhead through impact so that the club almost slides between the ground and ball, continuing down the slope as long as possible (Fig. 157). The ball will never pop up with tremendous height but it should get up sufficiently quickly to carry the bunker without running right through the green. It is a shot with definite limitations but one which may well get you out of one of golf's trickiest situations.

Recovering from the trees

Women as a rule hit the ball straighter than men. Firstly, we don't hit it so far, so bad direction isn't quite so obvious, and secondly, we know that we just can't afford to go in the rough so often because we can't recover as well. But even the very best golfer goes in the trees sometimes. The main thing is to recover well.

Firstly, try to assess just how much you can make up with your shot from the trees. It is no good playing a very risky shot if you don't stand to gain anything. It may be exciting, but it is much better to play a more conservative shot and be sure of getting out without risking getting yourself in a worse mess. Even if it means going out backwards or sideways this is better than leaving yourself in the trees. Sacrifice one shot – who knows you may make up for it on the green – rather than being too ambitious and losing several.

Having chosen your route out, have a few good practice swings, firstly watching the club both back and through to see if you are likely to meet with any tree limbs. Take this slowly and really plan the shot. To punch the ball out low, take a 3- or 4-iron, gripping well down the club and standing with the ball very nearly opposite your right foot. Keep the hands really well ahead of the ball, tipping the face over to reduce the loft as much as you need. From here, concentrate more than anything on watching the ball, keeping the weight favouring the left foot, and hitting down and through the ball.

159. The ball is very much below the feet, but by adopting a wide stance with the knees knocked inwards it is quite possible to swing to the ball and produce a reliable shot.

160. When the ground is bare the easiest way to tackle a bank round the green is just to putt the ball up and over it.

161. A slightly longer shot from bare ground is best tackled with a medium iron, hands well ahead to reduce the loft and just bumping it along and up the bank.

162. A good way of tackling a really steep bank when the flag is close to the edge of the green is to punch the ball straight into the bank, using a medium iron with the hands well leading.

163. The wedge is only really necessary when the ground is rough or the bank is at an angle to you. For the club golfer it is often the riskiest type of shot to play.

159

160

When you have nowhere to stand

One can sometimes be lucky enough for the ball to run through a bunker near the green, only to find that the shot you are left with is very nearly as awkward. If the ball finishes on the top of the bunker it can be difficult to find anywhere to stand; the beginner usually makes extra hard work of this and tries to stand in the bunker, so way below the ball. A much simpler way is to stand outside the bunker, turning your back on the target. Looking over your left shoulder, aim the club squarely on target and then, watching the ball very carefully, swing back and through on target. Even though you aren't aimed at the hole yourself it is still perfectly easy to send the ball in the right direction (Fig. 158). In fact it is even possible to hit the ball between your legs in this way. So don't give up in an awkward situation. Try to improvise and produce some kind of respectable shot.

The other awkward shot which comes under this heading is where one has to stand outside a bunker with the ball just in the edge of it, the feet 18 inches or more above the ball. The difficulty here is that if one purely tries to bend the knees to get down low enough to the ball, the knees get in the way of your swing. In this case spread your feet very well apart, knocking your knees inwards, not towards the ball, to bring yourself down closer to it. Practise taking the club up and down a couple of times to make sure the swing is possible and then pick the club up rather sharply, almost leaning more forwards and chopping down into the sand at the back of the ball (Fig. 159). Once you find a suitable way of standing the shot isn't as bad after all.

Playing to an elevated green

The difficult part about hitting to an elevated green is selecting the right club. Because the green is well above you, the ball touches down before it has finished its natural flight. It has therefore not reached the part of its trajectory where it is landing nearly vertically but instead shoots into the green while travelling in a much more forward direction. For this reason it

161

162

163

is very difficult to get a ball to stop well on a green well above you. What so easily happens is that one club always goes through the green, even though it may pitch fairly well to the front of it, where in taking one club less the ball actually pitches short and doesn't roll on. In playing uphill to a green, always try for as much height as possible on the shot, the better player producing this either by increasing the wrist action or playing the ball even further forward than usual. The main thing is to realize that a ball is always likely to run through an elevated green. Don't be fooled and play short the next time. If there is any trouble at the front of the green just be prepared to take enough club and get down in two from the back.

Playing to a green below you

In playing down to a green one finds just the reverse from playing up to a green. The ball now follows its full, natural flight and drops even more vertically than usual. If it pitches on the green a ball hit from a height will usually stop very quickly. The main danger here is that in being bold and playing right to the green, one may in fact underclub and so catch a downslope just in front of the cut surface. This is when there is most likelihood of going through. Rather than risk this, then, always pitch well onto a green in a basin and the ball will usually hold.

Playing to a banked green

Just because there is a bank in between your ball and the flag, don't assume that the only way over it is with a wedge. This, I feel, should be a last resort unless the lie is really good and grassy. If the lie is at all bare with fairly hard ground all the way to the edge of the green, by far the easiest shot is usually to putt the ball. Don't only treat the putter as a club to use on the green. You can make good use of it in this kind of situation. The only real danger is of leaving it short, so make sure that you give it enough to get up the hill and, as always, watch the ball intently (Fig. 160). For the same kind of shot, but from a rather longer distance, one wants to produce much the same thing, this time bumping the ball along with a 5- or 6-iron. The ball needs to be hit low so that it actually gets to the point of running, not jumping, as it goes up the bank. This time, set the hands very well ahead of

164–167. To hook a ball round an obstacle the left hand is set very much on top of the club with the right hand underneath it. The whole swing is aimed right of the obstacle, allowing the hands to roll over in the throughswing so that the clubface closes through impact.

164

165

the clubhead, ball off the right foot, so that the clubface is tipped well over to decrease the effective loft. This makes the ball travel very much forwards, not upwards, producing a shot which almost scuttles along and up the bank. Again the only danger is giving it too little, so don't try to cut things too fine, but give it sufficient to get on the green (Fig. 161).

When the flag is very close to a really steep, firm bank, the easiest way to get the ball to stop just over the bank is to actually bang the ball at the bank with a 5- or 6-iron, so that it hits the bank firmly, jumping almost vertically upwards and landing softly on the edge of the green.

Again the hands must be held well ahead of the clubhead, striking it firmly and confidently. In fact the firmness of the stroke is fairly unimportant because the harder one hits it, within reason, the higher the ball jumps, making very little difference to the actual distance it travels. This is an ideal shot particularly when the bank is very nearly, though not quite, vertical, or where there are any overhanging branches to interfere with an ordinary lofted shot (Fig. 162).

The wedge is, of course, the club to use in certain of these circumstances. But for the club golfer I don't think it should be the first choice. There is more to

go wrong with this kind of shot and the margins are usually rather finer. However, if the grass is at all rough or if the bank is at an angle to you one is virtually forced to cut the ball up and over it onto the green. In this case use the sand wedge, opening the clubface if necessary, and either play it with a stiff-wristed action, sacrificing a little extra height, or, if you are an experienced player, cutting it up with plenty of hand action. In either case, don't try to be too heroic in pitching right on the edge, but give yourself a little room for error. There is always the chance of holing a good putt (Fig. 163).

Putting from a bunker

Sometimes in playing from a shallow bunker around the green, the easiest shot, especially for the club golfer, is just to putt the ball out. To lend itself to this, the sand has to be very smooth and firm, with no noticeable lip to the bunker. In

this case remember not to touch the sand either in the address or backswing, but stroke the ball out smoothly. Don't chop onto it or the ball is likely to jump and get held up in the sand. Providing you are careful when to use this shot it can be a far safer one to play than either a chip or splash shot. Certainly when there is no lip to the bunker, many golfers don't feel happy with the rather long swing of the splash shot, perhaps feeling that it would be all too easy to send the ball far too far. In this case, the putt can be a good alternative.

Hooking out of trouble

Lastly, let's look at two shots for the really good player – hooking and slicing out of trouble. The first, the hook, is usually the

166

167

168

169

easier of the two. It is perhaps rather more difficult to judge exactly, but certainly easier to actually produce in some form or another. One can put considerably more hook on a ball with a given club than slice. Let's look at a shot to be hooked around the trees. The first point is to start the ball right of the obstacle, so aiming out well to the right with the feet and shoulders. The idea is then to swing in this direction, closing the clubface by impact so that the clubface aims considerably left. To induce this, the left hand is put well on top of the club, all four knuckles showing, with the right completely under the club. Have a few practice swings, feeling that just before impact the right hand rolls over the left, the wrists beginning to cross so that the clubface is definitely closed. In doing this the swing will feel

168–170. To slice a ball round an obstacle the right hand is kept very much on top in the grip, aiming the whole swing left of the obstacle and then holding the clubface open through impact to impart the necessary sidespin.

very flat around the body. Then, with the ball, concentrate on starting it out in the right direction, really rolling the hands and clubface over to produce plenty of hook (Figs. 164–167).

Slicing around trouble

The amount of slice one is likely to get with any club is usually much less than the hook one can produce. This is because much of the spin is taken up with producing height – the slice nearly always taking up added height and the hook going off much lower. Faced with a tree bang in

170

my line I would therefore usually opt for hooking around it, the bend in this direction being rather easier to exaggerate. To produce a slicing shot the first consideration once again should be the initial direction, making certain that one aims sufficiently far left with the stance. The left hand grip can then be altered to show perhaps only one knuckle, with the right hand – the more important of the two – folded well over with the 'V' to the left shoulder. The feeling is then of taking the club up steeply outside the line of the shot, in other words well away from the body, feeling that the clubface rolls slightly open, toe of the clubhead leading. In the downswing the club cuts across the line of the shot – from 'out-to-in' – keeping the clubface held open. If one can actually think of the clubface, all the better; if not, the grip will usually take care of this to a certain extent, producing quite a bend on the ball from left to right (Figs. 168–170).

14 THINK YOUR WAY TO BETTER GOLF

Most ball games involve some kind of thinking and tactics – planning ahead or outwitting your opponent. Golf, perhaps, requires almost more than any other. The time factor in golf makes it very much a thinking game. One doesn't have to hit any shot from instinct or purely with a reflexive reaction. Instead one can really take time to consider the shot quite carefully before executing it. As far as technique and the swing goes, this is possibly one of the main drawbacks for the average golfer. If the ball had to be hit without too much time for thinking – in other words, if one were back to a moving ball situation – there are many players who would possibly develop better swings and become less confused about the mechanics of the swing. Then, of course, there are others who hit it as though it were a moving ball, never giving a moment's thought to what is wanted from the swing or, in fact, from the shot itself!

To make the very best of one's swing the amount of thought which goes into it has to strike a happy medium. One needs to take plenty of time with actually planning the shot, choosing a definite target, assessing the distance, judging the strength of the wind, looking at the lie, selecting the club, aiming correctly and so on, but then in the swing one has to limit the thinking to a very few concrete thoughts and ideas. As a rule, I think, the average golfer spends far too little time on the first of these two processes, very rarely taking sufficient time to plan the actual shot. With the swing, on the other hand, she often tries to think of far too much. In this chapter let's look at the way in which one needs to approach each shot, both from the point of view of planning it and also of producing your best swing whatever the situation.

Every shot counts the same

One of the weaknesses of most golfers is that they want to hit the ball as far as possible on each shot, even at the risk of going into trouble. I don't mean that they try to hit the ball too hard, for the problem with most women golfers is to get them to be sufficiently aggressive. No, what I mean is that they tend to resort to the longest clubs in every case to make progress up the fairway, instead of being rather more conservative and choosing a club for safety. Shots don't count as halves in golf; if you can't reach a green in one shot then it is going to take you two, and these two count just the same whether you hit a 3-wood and a wedge or a 4-iron and an 8-iron. I know the longer handicap player feels more secure the closer she gets to the green – believe you me, so does the professional – but it is often very much better to play for position than to go for maximum length.

On a particularly tight hole I think the question to ask is always 'How many shots do I need to reach the green?' Obviously the longer handicap player may stand on the tee and not really know how many she needs, but once one gets within two or three shots of the green – for the good golfer, right from the tee – it is possible to start planning ahead.

If you stand to reach the green either with one full shot or with two full shots, then by all means play for maximum length. But if it seems likely that either your first shot or your first and second shots are going to leave you comfortably short of the green, really weigh up the problem of the rough, the lie or any other trouble. If there is an out of bounds fence close to one side of the fairway, if there are bunkers obviously waiting to catch you or if your lie is poor, be prepared to play the hole in easy stages. It is always much better to take a shorter club and hit it confidently up the fairway than to take a 2- or 3-wood and hit it rather half-heartedly. The main point is to remember that two shots count as two shots, and three shots count as three shots with whichever clubs and in whatever order you play them.

Keeping away from trouble

Especially on British courses, bunkers, ditches or banks of heather across the fairway tend to be a problem for the club golfer. The number who play blindly into cross bunkers in particular is staggering. Obviously one cannot make any really hard and fast rule about when to play short and when to go for the carry, but I think one has to look at the likelihood of both success and failure as well as the rewards and penalties one faces. Very often I find club golfers take a risk in going for a carry when they stand to lose a great deal and don't stand to gain very much. If the row of bunkers is right in front of the green, then it is almost always worth going for the carry. Should one land in the bunker, the problem of getting out onto the green is comparatively small and one is no worse off than playing short. On the other hand, if the bunkers are quite a way from the green, say around 40 yards, one runs the risk of not being able to get out and onto the green. Here the risks are a little greater, and I would always be rather more hesitant about going for the carry. Once the row of bunkers is much further from the green, there may be little to be gained.

Even if one does get the carry one is unlikely to get the green itself; on the other hand if one goes in the bunker then the chances of getting out and onto the green are extremely slim. So one really does have to look at this thoroughly. All right, take the risk, but do you gain anything if you pull off the shot? And what are the penalties if you don't?

The fairway bunkers which face one from the tee also need careful consideration. Supposing there is a bunker to one or both sides of the fairway, just the length of my drive, and obviously making the hole very narrow; now what should I do? First let's assume the hole is a short par-4. Now instead of hitting a rather risky drive and perhaps a 9-iron I can be much safer in hitting a 4-wood, short of any bunkers, followed by a 7- or 8-iron, or even a 2-iron and 6-iron. The 6-iron is only a little more diffi-

cult to hit to the green than the 9 and I don't risk going in the bunker and not being able to reach the green in two. But supposing the hole is a long par-4 or short par-5 and I can just reach it with a driver and 3-wood. Now it is certainly worth hitting my driver. If I took the 4-wood and played short I wouldn't be able to reach the green in two anyway. Here the risk is worth taking. If I do go in the bunker I can probably recover far enough to be able to get home with the third shot so the penalties are comparatively small.

One cannot lay down any set rules on planning a hole in this way. On an awkward par-4 or par-5, four professionals may see and plan it in four different ways. But what they all have in common is that they *think* out the hole and plan it the way that seems most sensible to them.

Playing for position

To a certain extent, of course, it is much easier for the good golfer to plan a hole, but there is a great deal even the longest handicap players can do in getting into the right type of positions on the course. If you look carefully at most holes, there is a definite right side and wrong side for playing into the green, sometimes varying according to where the flag is. If the green is heavily bunkered to the front on one side, for example, it rather dictates that one attacks the green from the other side of the fairway. Very often, in fact, one is almost better off in the edge of the rough on one side of the hole than being nicely down the

centre or other side of the fairway. Longer handicap and middle handicap players on the whole are not good at positioning themselves in this way. And it is not just because they are at the mercy of their swings rather more than the better player. No, the majority of medium handicap women golfers can hit the ball very, very straight and are quite capable of positioning themselves perfectly. It is the shot before the one to the green which can make all the difference. At this stage say to yourself, 'Now where do I want to approach the green from? Is my easiest shot from the left or from the right, or should I just

play for the centre of the fairway?' Don't just aim straight at the flag all the time.

Setting up for the drive
For the lower handicap golfer it is the positioning of the drive which can be so vital. Partly, of course, one has to be concerned on many holes with just going for the safest part of the fairway, but where the green and even the position of the flag does lend itself better to one kind of approach, the drive should be played with the idea of leaving just this shot. Obviously one isn't going to find the right position every time but there are definite ways of approaching the

tee shot to make this much more likely.

If you look at a group of top class golfers walking onto the tee, their whole approach is usually entirely different from that of a group of club players. The club golfer usually just tees up on the closest part of the tee, following everyone else, without really looking at the shot to be played. On the other hand, the professional usually takes particular trouble with choosing the right spot on the tee, not only ensuring that it is level, but looking at the type of shot it gives. On a wide tee, one can get a completely different impression of the hole from one side to the other. If one tees up very much on the right of the tee and then aims at the centre of the fairway one is turned somewhat towards the left side of the hole and away from any trouble on the right. On the other hand, if one tees up far

over to the left of the tee one is naturally forced to aim more towards the right side of the hole in trying for the centre of the fairway. If, therefore, all the trouble on any hole is down the left of the fairway it is generally better to tee up well over to the left, meaning that one can be aimed away from this in driving for the centre of the fairway. So if the trouble is all down one side, start on that side of the tee and turn away from it.

Length isn't everything

The second way in which one can play for position is in resorting once more to a shorter shot than is possible. In Britain and other countries where the small ball is played, stopping the ball on the green with a half or three-quarter length wedge shot is often very much more difficult than holding the green with a full

shot. Not only this, but the full shot is often easier to judge for distance. In this case, don't necessarily take the driver off the tee or a wood for the fairway shot for the par-5 but try to leave yourself the easiest possible shot into the green even if it means sacrificing a little distance. A downhill lie is something else to avoid where you can. Once again, think in terms of hitting a 3-wood from the tee and leaving yourself a flat stance with a 9-iron, rather than hitting the driver and finding yourself hitting a half or three-quarter wedge from a treacherous stance. On the short par-4s and par-5s in particular, position can be everything. On a good course this is usually the whole feature of this type of hole. It doesn't have to be long to be difficult and the hole is often designed to outwit you into positioning the ball badly.

Gambling versus the percentage shot

Of course, thinking correctly doesn't guarantee you aren't going to get into trouble. But because one may get into the rough or trees doesn't mean it is time to stop this logical thought and resort to stupidity. It is so easy to get into trouble and then try desperately to make up ground, getting into a worse and worse mess with every blow. It is so tempting to take the 4-wood in the hopes of pulling off a miraculous shot, at the best still leaving a full wedge to the green, and at the worse, who knows? How much better to take the wedge from the rough and the 4-wood to the green, or a 7-iron out and a 5-iron on with very little chance of doing anything disastrous. The only time to be

ambitious is where it is actually possible to reach the green. Even here, though, one is often better to be a little more cautious and play a slightly shorter club, perhaps being better off safely just short than flirting with the bunkers around the green. Always play within your capabilities and settle for dropping one shot, rather than gambling and losing four or five instead. If you recover conservatively it often seems to be just the time you roll in a good putt; the hole where everything goes wrong is usually the one you three-putt to add to the trouble.

Personality and risk taking

Of course, in this type of situation the individual personality

of the golfer comes into play. Some are natural gamblers and are motivated very much by the thought of bringing off the spectacular, discounting any possible idea of failure. Others are not gamblers at heart; they tend to be motivated more by not wanting to fail with any shot than by thoughts of outstanding success with it. In some ways it is never easy to change this pattern. The first type of player will nearly always take undue risks and always take a gamble; her scores usually tend to fluctuate rather more, with birdies and pars when the gamble pays off, but eights and nines often cropping up for almost no reason. The second type of player is much more likely to produce a steadier type of scoring, getting out of trouble less spectacularly and having fewer bad holes in her rounds of golf. In some ways it is difficult to say which is better. The first type of golfer often goes on to have more really exceptional rounds and wins but the second builds up a more consistent scoring pattern, often, perhaps, being better at stroke play where the other is better in matchplay.

Percentage golf

Whichever type of golfer one is, the important point is to take time to consider the consequences of any shot, both when it is played perfectly and less than perfectly. In this way it is possible to play 'percentage golf' – in other words playing, not for the shot which is 100 per cent perfect, but the one which is 80 or 90 per cent perfect, according to ability. This gives a safety margin for anything to go wrong.

In any round the professional can usually pick out just a very small number of shots executed absolutely perfectly – perhaps three or four. The number is terribly small – probably surprisingly small to the longer handicap. The rest may all feel 95 per cent perfect, but anyone watching can hardly distinguish those few perfect ones from the rest of the round. This is because the professional is experienced at allowing for this minute margin of error. He or she doesn't often aim for a shot which must be 100 per cent perfect to work and where anything less means trouble. No, there is nearly always a safety margin. If the flag is positioned right round behind a bunker, perhaps 10 feet over it, the professional is unlikely to play for the flag except from relatively close range. He won't aim for the flag with a 2-iron shot or even, on the whole, with a 5- or 6-iron. Instead he plays the safe percentage shot to the centre of the green or else makes sure he has sufficient club to carry well over the bunker.

Play within your capabilities

The club golfer is nearly always even more ambitious than the professional and plays directly for the flag on almost every shot. The whole idea of tucking the flag right behind or beside a bunker is to draw you into the sand and many golfers fall into this kind of trap time after time. The shot may be 95 per cent perfect, beautifully struck, a good length and very nearly dead straight, but if you haven't played the percentage shot it is likely to be in trouble. The professional, by contrast, will probably just have aimed for the centre of the green or the appropriate quarter of the green and be putting for a birdie. So with any long shot don't necessarily hit for the flag. You aren't going to produce perfect shots everytime by any means so don't attempt shots which require perfection.

Follow this same kind of logic round the green as well. Now if the shot facing you is a difficult one, from a bunker or a bare lie, the chances are you aren't going to get within certain one-putt range. If you can get within 8 feet that is probably very satisfactory, and it doesn't really matter whether this 8 feet is to the left, to the right, short or past the flag. Very often it is possible to aim slightly to one side of the hole and have a very much easier shot to play than in going straight for the flag. There may be the edge of a bunker in your way, a bank, rough grass, high lip of a bunker. Try to look at the possibilities of giving yourself an easier shot than the one straight for the flag. You want to get as close to the flag as possible. But don't try to bring off the impossible or the most difficult shot if there are other alternatives. If you try for the perfect shot it *might* come off but you might finish 30 feet past or 30 feet short. If there is an alternative way of safely finishing 6 feet to the side, take it. This is percentage golf, the way the tournament golfer will usually play.

Positive thinking and imagery

Now, in talking about percentage golf, the last thing I want to encourage is negative thinking. Having said that the tournament golfer allows for a minute margin of error in many shots, I don't mean that she is ever contemplating a poorly struck shot. Far from it. Having decided on the type of shot and made allowances in this choice for any slight error, her whole

attitude to hitting the ball must be entirely positive.

The first stage is to choose a definite target. One must never look at the green and just think of missing all the bunkers, or look at the fairway and think of steering the ball between the rough on the left and trees on the right. This is far too negative. Instead one must pick out a really positive target, setting one's sights only on hitting to this, without thinking any further of the trouble.

Visualizing the shot

The next stage is to visualize the whole shot, having a full dress rehearsal, as it were, in the practice swing and imagining the flight of the ball correctly on target. The more experienced one becomes, the easier it is to do this whole preparatory stage in the mind; in many instances the professional may not include a physical practice swing but the mental preparation is always there. She knows in her mind's eye just what she wants in the swing and in the shot, and the more vivid and more positive this can be, the greater her chance of success.

The fact that this thinking process must be positive is vital. Think of it in this way. The pictures held in the mind are transmitted through to the muscles; the muscles in turn see this set of pictures as instructions and as far as possible act upon them. The better the player the greater is this 'muscle memory.' In fact the good player gets to the stage where a full range of shots is possible, hardly consciously adjusting stance or swing, but purely relying on the mental instructions. This is great; it

means that one can have a complete repertoire of shots at hand to manoeuvre one's way around the course. But, it can equally work against you. This is where we get the negative image. Supposing, for example, I am faced with a drive down a rather narrow fairway with out of bounds along the right. Now if I look along the hole and think to myself, 'Don't slice whatever you do,' the picture of the slice is in my mind. The fact that the slice is just what I don't want can't be transmitted to the muscles. They immediately take the idea of the slice to be a positive set of instructions and in all good faith do their very best to give me just the slice I was trying so hard to avoid.

Everything in visualizing shots or actions must be positive; certainly this is the way in which the muscles will respond to them. If you imagine the delicate pitch shot dropping short into the bunker, the chances are that is just what it will do. If you see a 4-foot putt pulled away to the left of the hole, it will pull away to the left. If you stand on the tee and imagine the ball duck-hooking into a gorse bush you don't stand a great deal of chance of hitting it straight down the fairway. Certainly for the better player it is the mental picture of the swing and shot which is likely to be the controlling factor with awkward or disliked shots. The long handicap player is, perhaps, less governed by this mental picture of each shot, for the brain and muscles don't co-ordinate quite as naturally, but it is still very, very vital to picture the swing, and picture the shot vividly before physically executing it.

Imagery and ability

This phenomenon of imagery – of being able to picture things in the mind – is, or can be, a very important one to the golfer. All the senses are active in this respect to a different degree; one can imagine tastes, or hear sounds in the mind, or 'feel' the texture of things, 'see' vivid pictures or imagine the body in different types of movements and positions. The ability to conjure up images and the control one has over them varies enormously from one individual to another; some people, in fact, have no concept of imagery at all with certain senses, even in the visual sense which, as a rule, is the strongest or one of the strongest. In golf we are really concerned with two senses – visual images and body movement images. Good golfers, as a rule, appear to have a strong ability in the sense of movement. This really boils down to what one generally calls 'co-ordination' – great control over the body and limbs. People with this type of ability can usually look at someone else doing a physical action and relate it so that they can 'see' themselves doing the action. In golf the player who finds the game difficult is often poor in this type of ability, finding it terribly hard to imitate and also to feel the right kind of movements in the limbs. The player who has very little sense of body movement in this way is bound to be hampered to an extent in golf; she is probably less able to judge shots well or to adapt the swing easily. If one can improve this ability and make it more vivid, then mental practice can become a very large part of the game.

Mental practice

For the golfer with a strong sense of imagery it is often possible to get very nearly as much benefit from mental practice as from physical striking of the ball. One can groove actions in the swing by repeating them over and over in the mind; one can overcome difficulties with certain shots by playing them again and again mentally; one can destroy the pattern of hooking by repeating the idea of slicing; one can think of putt after putt of 4 feet going straight in the cup and mentally strengthen the putting stroke and confidence. Just before the shot is made one can see the flight of the ball, feeling every important action of the swing, and so making it very much more likely to happen physically. If time for practice is limited then a few minutes a day just thinking about the swing and trying to keep the feeling of the correct actions in the mind is a fairly good substitute. It is a good idea, too, to imagine the way in which you want to play round the course, making it much easier to produce the right type of positive images in actual play. Imagery in both the visual and body movement senses can be important to the golfer, both as a way of improving the swing and in making the very best of that swing round the course. Good golfers, as a rule, produce the swing and shot they want because they 'feel' the swing and 'see' the shot very clearly before actually executing it.

What to think of in the swing

The point to realize about the actual golf swing is that it takes a very short time, something like 2 or 3 seconds. In this time it just isn't possible to think of very many things. One has to limit these to perhaps three or four. On the whole I think club golfers perhaps tend to think of too much, confusing themselves and neglecting the most important things. By all means in practice work on several points of theory but once you get out on the course try to pick out just a few concrete ideas for each shot. Much of the work can really be done in the practice swing. Here one can groove the right actions and think of rather more things. One hasn't got to think of watching the ball or generating quite so much speed so here is the real time to organize the thoughts for the swing. Get as much as you can out of the practice swing, and then again in the set-up. By this time everything you want from the swing should be carefully planned.

Fix in your mind the three or four ideas that are going to be used in the swing. Itemize them carefully to yourself before the swing ever starts. 'One, turn your shoulders; two, stay down and watch the ball; three, grip firmly; four, produce a firm, balanced followthrough.' Prepare all this at address and in the practice swing. Having chosen the right club and lined up the shot, try to forget all about this. You don't want to have anything else in mind but the three or four definite ideas you chose for the swing. If you make room for any kind of uncertainty about the clubbing or the troubles down the fairway your mind can't be entirely on striking the ball as it should be. So at this stage, block out every other thought. Forget about the club. Forget about the score. Forget about the bunkers. Just think of making the best looking swing you can, watching the ball and producing a firm, positive finish to the swing.

The aim of the game – scoring

When one comes to the final analysis of one's golf, it isn't how one strikes the ball, or how good one looks doing it, or how far one hits, or how well one putts, that really matters. It is how few shots one takes to go round the course. Scoring is, or should be, the aim of everything you do on the course. The ability to score well is something quite separate from everything one learns on the technique of the swing. With the true professional champion there is nothing separating the ability to strike the ball or to play the finesse shots from the way in which a hundred other professionals play. There is just that something extra which dictates that a particular golfer consistently scores that little bit better than the rest. Part of it is determination; part of it is confidence; part of it is a question of attitude – trying hard without putting unnecessary pressure on oneself. But then again there is an art to scoring which can definitely be learnt and developed, not necessarily making one a champion, of course, but making one score at least as well if not better than the outward appearance of one's swing and ability. A great deal of this goes along with better thinking and planning of the holes, negotiating your way round trouble, positioning the ball well and playing 'percentage golf.' However, there is still a great deal one can do in creating the right attitude towards scoring, stringing all the shots into a good final score for the course.

Play each shot for itself

My first advice is to forget both the par of the hole and your score. Play each shot for itself to the best of your ability, regardless of what has gone before. If you are doing well, don't try to steer the ball safely the rest of the way, and if things have gone badly don't try to make up for them with shots you wouldn't normally attempt. Try to play each shot the same whether you are four under par or eight over par, or whether you had a three or a nine on the hole before. If you have a bad drive or a lost ball, don't attack the next shot in any different way from normal.

Just try to let the score happen by putting together shot after shot after shot, never looking back but only planning ahead for the hole facing you. Never even look beyond that.

Don't expect perfection

Also try to resign yourself to the fact that you are going to have some less than perfect shots in every round. If you are a long handicap player then you are probably going to have some extremely bad shots in every round, but don't let these effect the way in which you go on playing. If the round hasn't started well it doesn't mean it will go badly the rest of the way. You are going to have that quota of poor shots and whether these all come in the first few holes or the last few makes no difference to the final score – if, that is, you can forget about them or at least not bother about them. On the law of averages, those bad shots are going to crop up somewhere, and they can just as easily crop up on the first, second and third as anywhere else on the round. It is no indication of what is going to follow. The total score is the one that matters, and whether this is made up of an outward half of forty-five and an inward one of thirty-five or vice versa makes no difference at all. The more and more experienced one becomes as a golfer, the easier it is to realize just what can happen on a golf course, the extraordinary patterns of scoring produced and the unlikely sequences of birdies and eagles. Anything is possible in scoring, so just keep plodding away and let the score look after itself.

Matchplay – play for the figures

Matchplay is a very different type of mental test from stroke play. Golfers who win at one don't necessarily win at the other. The mental side, I suppose, comes into matchplay rather more. In this case every fault you make and hole you lose not only tends to discourage you, but tends to encourage your opponent, almost doubling the effect. The ideal way to treat matchplay is to think of it in much the same way as a medal round, just stringing the shots together as well as possible and letting the score take shape. Play the course and not the opponent. Never change the way you play a hole because of something your opponent has done, unless she has obviously got into terrible trouble and you really do have three or four shots in hand. Remember that she can just as easily sink a chip shot while you three-putt. So don't take things for granted. Concentrate on getting your own figures and let her worry about getting hers. Don't think about her score until you are on the green and it is obvious what is left for you to do. Just keep playing for the figures and the wins will follow.

Once again think in terms of a certain quota of good and bad, this time in terms of the number of wins and losses. Some holes you are going to win and some you are going to lose. You can just as easily lose the first four as any on the course, but if you can lose four like this, so can your opponent. Enormous changes can take place in matchplay. The player who is leading often makes the great mistake of relaxing, she loses one or two holes of the lead and all of a sudden feels the match is sliding away. Don't let this happen. Firstly, if you are in the lead never ease up. Never feel even the slightest bit sorry for an opponent. She isn't going to feel sorry for you even if she wins all those holes back. So don't take anything for granted until the match is won or lost. Secondly, never worry if the lead does begin to slip. If you are one up it doesn't matter whether four holes ago you were five up or three down. One up is one up.

Don't anticipate a winning hole

Take a definitely positive approach towards your opponent's play. When you are playing your own shot never think what she is likely to do or what she isn't likely to do. Play your own shot and never mind hers. But when she is playing always assume she will produce her best possible shot. Tell yourself she will hole every putt or lay every approach shot close or hit every drive down the centre of the fairway. Never assume or hope she will hit a bad shot or miss a putt. If you think like this you immediately become deflated or discouraged if she produces a great shot. If you look upon it the other way and expect her not to make errors, everytime she does it gives you a tremendous psychological lift. If she produces a great shot it was really all you were expecting. So don't anticipate errors from your opponent, only anticipate good shots. So think positively both for yourself and your opponent, just playing the course and playing for the figures and letting the score take care of itself.

So there it is, the mental side of golf. There is a great deal to learn and understand; for some it is much more difficult than the actual golf swing and for others it is very much easier. Whatever standard of golfer one becomes, however, it is often the difference between thinking well and thinking badly which determines the score that finally goes down on the card, and it is the score, after all, that really counts.

15 A CHAPTER FOR THE BEGINNER

The main problem about golf is that it is a very difficult game to learn. It isn't like many games which one can at least enjoy almost immediately. No, good tuition and plenty of it is essential in taking up golf. There is a great deal to learn so that for the beginner the first year or couple of years may seem rather frustrating and a little disappointing. But it is the very difficulty of this initial period which makes golf such a fascinating sport. Having gone through hours of struggling and practice it all seems very much more rewarding when things *do* go well. Perhaps this is the true charm of golf.

There is a lot to learn. There is no getting away from this – not just in the swing, but with all the technical terms and types of competitions, handicaps and rules, all of which seem terribly confusing. So here, then, is a chapter for the complete beginner. I don't confess to packing absolutely everything you need to know into this chapter, but it should at least set you well on your way with most of the knowledge you need for joining and taking an active part in a golf club.

The set of clubs

First let's take a look at the set of clubs; you certainly won't need all of them as a beginner and two or three of them you probably never will use; they are really only clubs for the international golfer.

The set consists of two basic kinds of clubs – the woods and irons. Very logically the woods have wood (or simulated wood) heads and the irons have iron (steel) heads. The set of clubs is designed to produce a full range of different heights and lengths of shots, firstly through the angle of the clubface – the scored part at the front of the head – and secondly through variations in the length of the clubs. Through both the woods and irons the higher the number of the club the shorter the shaft and more angled the clubface, so that the higher the ball is likely to rise and shorter distance it travels (Figs. 171 and 172).

The woods

The woods, then, are graded from 1 to 5, though occasionally even higher than this; the driver, which is the usual name for the 1-wood, having the least angled or 'lofted' face and the longest shaft of any in the set. This then is designed to hit the ball to the maximum distance, producing a long, low trajectory. As we go up through the 2-, 3-, 4- and 5-woods the shaft gets shorter, half an inch at a time, while the clubface gets more and more lofted, so that with the woods we have five different types of shot; the longest and lowest with the

171. The full range of clubs – the woods from 1 to 5 and the irons from 1 to sand wedge, plus the putter. Of these clubs the 1-iron is a specialist club for the top class international golfer, while the 2-iron is also a relatively uncommon club in women's golf. The maximum number of clubs any golfer can include in her set is fourteen, so that the usual combination is four woods, plus the irons from 3 to sand wedge and the putter. A beginner by no means needs all these clubs, but can start with perhaps four or five of them, adding others as she becomes more proficient at the game.

130 The Complete Woman Golfer

driver and shortest and highest with the 5-wood. The woods, however, are our power clubs and even the 5-wood is designed to produce a comparatively long shot.

The irons

As we move on to the irons we start with the 1- and 2-irons which are two clubs only really for the top class woman golfer – the 2-iron having some use by good women golfers but the 1-iron being a somewhat specialist club, usually only carried in exceptional conditions by top class tournament players. So you can forget about these two for the time being! The irons which you are likely to use range from the 3 all the way up to the 10, often known as the pitching wedge, plus the sand wedge, which is really the equivalent of the 11-iron. Again the clubs get shorter and shorter by half an inch between adjacent clubs and in so doing become more and more lofted. The 3-iron produces the longest, lowest shot of the irons

and, despite the several inches difference in length between it and the 5-wood, produces a shot of very much the same distance, perhaps 10 yards shorter. The 10-iron and sand wedge give the shortest, highest shots of the set.

I am often asked at this stage how far each club should hit the ball. This is really impossible to say. I can tell you how far I or the majority of women professionals hit the ball, but this doesn't really have any meaning for the beginner. I probably hit the ball about 230 yards with my driver; as a beginner you will be more likely to hit it say 100 or 110 yards. Each club does not produce guaranteed distance; the set of clubs produces a set of relative distances. So, for example, I find that I have a 10-yard gap between adjacent clubs; you on the other hand as a beginner may only find 4 or 5 yards between clubs. The important point is that the clubs give you a range of shots. As you play more your overall distance will improve; and as your distance im-

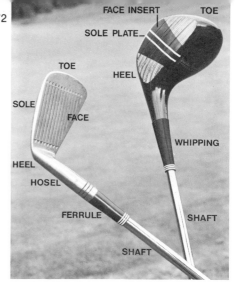

172. The parts of a wood and an iron.

proves so you will gradually need more and more of the clubs in the set. At first all you really need, to be able to start on all the shots in golf, is a wood, two irons and finally a putter. This is the club used on the green – and in some cases around the green – designed not to loft the ball, but to roll it along the ground into the hole. This is a short shafted club with virtually no loft on the face, and although with older clubs the putter may have some number, often 9 or 10 on the bottom of it, it will easily stand out as being different from the other irons.

The course

From looking at the set of clubs let's move on to talk about the golf course itself. A golf course almost always consists of either eighteen or nine holes, varying in length from about 90 yards to 550 yards, starting each at the tee and playing along the fairway to the green and from there into the hole.

Areas of the course

There are really four different areas of the course to concern ourselves with. Firstly, there is the tee, which is the start of each

hole and is the only part of the course where the ball can be teed up on a tee-peg and the lie of the ball improved by picking any grass which is growing or by treading down the ground. The second is the hazard area of the course, which includes sand bunkers and ditches or ponds, described as 'water hazards.' In these you cannot ground the club, in other words touch the ground at address, nor remove any 'loose impediments' such as twigs and leaves, which might be in the way. The third area is

known as 'through the green' which is the whole area of the course other than hazards, and the tee and green of the hole being played. This includes the cut part of the fairway and the rough – the long grass bordering the fairway – for the rules of golf treat this as one and the same. Lastly, there is the green – the finely manicured putting surface – in which the hole is cut. On this area you may mark the position of the ball with a coin or similar object and clean it to help in putting the ball.

Marker's Score	Hole	Yards	Par	Stroke Index	Player's Gross Score	Result	Marker's Score	Hole	Yards	Par	Stroke Index	Player's Gross Score	Result
	1	457	5	10				10	405	5	1		
	2	328	4	6				11	352	4	11		
	3	288	4	18				12	436	5	5		
	4	134	3	12				13	180	3	17		
	5	405	4	2				14	400	4	3		
	6	120	3	16				15	246	4	13		
	7	300	4	8				16	170	3	7		
	8	428	5	4				17	214	4	15		
	9	303	4	14				18	350	4	9		

S.S.S. 72 — LADIES' CARD — Handicap.................

Date................. Competition................. Strokes Received.............
Player.................

| OUT | | 2763 | 36 | | | | IN | | 2753 | 36 | | | |

| OUT | | 2763 | 36 |
| TOTAL | | 5516 | 72 |

HANDICAP

NET SCORE (Medal)

RESULT (Bogey Stableford)

Marker's Signature ....
Player's Signature ....
Strokes are to be taken at those Holes opposite which the figure is equal to or less than the total Handicap Allowance.
In Bogey play put + for win, − for lost, and 0 for halved in Result Column.
In Stableford play put points scored in result column.
In Medal play result column to be left blank.

173. A typical ladies' scorecard.

ance – a total of five shots. There is a certain degree of overlap in these pars, so that a hole of 210 yards, for example, might be either a par-3 or par-4 according to the positions of bunkers, general slope of the ground and general difficulty. For this reason both the length of the hole and the par allotted to it are given on the card of the course for you to keep your score on (Fig. 173).

So each hole has a par, and when these are added together for all eighteen holes (adding each twice for a nine-hole course) we have a total somewhere between 66 and 76 as a rule. This total par is the measure of the whole course from which one's standard of play and handicap can be assessed. The top class player taken as the standard for this score we call a 'scratch player'. She is expected to complete the course in the total par score and so we refer to this as the 'standard scratch score' or 'par' for the course.

Par and standard scratch

Each of these eighteen holes is given a 'par', which is the number of shots in which a really top class player would be expected to complete it, from the tee into the hole. In parts of the world, Britain included, this term 'par' is still referred to as 'bogey', but because in America 'bogey' is entirely different from the original meaning of it, the term is gradually dying out in this context, so from now on let's refer to this rating as 'par'.

A par-3 hole is anything in length up to about 225 yards; a good player should expect to reach this green in one shot and is then given an allowance of two putts to hole the ball, giving a total of three shots. A par-4 hole is anything from around 200 to 420 yards. The good player should reach the green in two long shots plus the two putt allowance – four shots in all. And lastly the par-5 is anything from between around 400 and 550 yards – our good player needing three long shots onto the green plus the two putt allow-

Handicaps

Let's assume we have a course where the standard scratch score is 72 – probably consisting of ten par-4 holes, four par-3 holes and four par-5 holes. A player, probably of international standard, whose average of her best scores is 72 would be given a handicap of scratch.

A player whose best scores averaged 79 would be assessed as 7 handicap; her standard being seven over the standard scratch of 72 for this course. This would make her one of the best players in any club and just near the fringe of national tournament standard.

Next let's take the 18 handicap player; her average best score would be 90 – 18 over the standard scratch – and would probably put her in the club second team. All these players we call silver division players – those with handicaps up to 18. From 19 upwards we have the bronze division.

So in the bronze division we have players whose scores average from 91 upwards; an average of 96 giving a handicap of 24 i.e., 96 less 72, an average of 102 giving a 30 handicap and so on up to 36 – the maximum handicap for ladies. This is the hand-

icap the beginner is given after marking her first cards; even if her scores are well up in the hundreds her handicap is 36 and remains so until she can better 108, i.e. 72 plus 36, when it starts to reduce.

The actual method of handicapping varies from one country to another, in the number of cards one is expected to complete within a year and in the exact method of computing them, but what any handicap system does mean is that players of all standards can compete together to give all an equal chance of winning.

Medal play

The first type of competition is the 'medal' or 'stroke play' round; here each player adds up her scores on each hole to give her total score for the course. This score we call the 'gross' score. Any prize given for the lowest gross score is known as the 'scratch prize' – the prize for the best play of the day regardless of handicap.

After the gross score is totalled the player's handicap is subtracted from this to give the 'nett' score, so, for example, if a 22 handicap player goes round in 97 her gross score is 97 and her nett score 75, i.e., 97 less 22. In any handicap stroke competition the lowest of these nett scores wins, so giving each player an equal chance.

Matchplay

Secondly, let's take a match between two players with handicaps 8 and 28. This is purely a match between the two players rather than a medal competition in which all the players are competing against everyone else. Here the players play a hole by hole game and are not concerned with the total score for the course. The lower score on each hole wins that hole, but to give the 28 handicap player a fair chance the 8 handicap would give the 28 player a number of 'strokes' or 'shots'. This number is assessed as three-quarters of the difference in their handicaps, i.e. ¾(28–8) = 15; the 28 handicap player would receive fifteen strokes. This means that on fifteen holes on the course the 28 handicap deducts one stroke from her actual score before matching scores with her opponent. So on the first hole if she receives a stroke and takes five shots she subtracts the stroke giving her a nett score of four. If the 8 handicap player takes four they halve the hole and the score is 'all square'. Supposing on the second the 28 handicap receives another stroke and both players score five, her nett score of four would win the hole and she would become one up. If she lost the next hole she would return to all square and if she lost the next she would become 1 down and the opponent would then become 1 up. At the end of each hole it is generally accepted etiquette for the player who is down to state the score. The match then finishes when one player is sufficient holes up that even if she lost all the remaining ones the opponent could not pull back to all square. As an example, if one player became three up after sixteen holes there would only be two holes remaining, and even if the opponent won these she would still be one down at the finish. We say, therefore, that the player has won by '3 up and 2 holes to play' which is abbreviated '3 and 2'.

Receiving your strokes

So in matchplay where do you receive strokes? Having assessed the number, i.e., three-quarters of the handicap difference – let's assume this gives the same difference of 15 – look at the scorecard for the column marked 'stroke index'. Our player would receive a stroke on each hole with a number 15 or less beside it, making a total of 15 holes. On the card shown here this would be on every hole except the third, sixth and thirteenth (Fig. 173).

Again a 12 handicap player playing the 8 handicap would receive ¾(12–8), i.e., 3 strokes taken at those holes marked 1, 2 and 3 in the stroke index, this time on the fifth, tenth and fourteenth. Anyone receiving more than 18 strokes would receive a stroke on every hole and would then take an additional one starting with stroke index 1, 2, 3 and so on, in other words with this card taking 2 strokes on the fifth, tenth and fourteenth.

Other competitions

These two forms of play, matchplay and medal or stroke play, are the main forms of competition. There are others, however, which you will gradually come across as you begin to join in the activities of your club. Play is not always only in pairs, correctly known as 'singles' but can also be in groups of three or four. The format for a three ball is usually either with each player marking a medal card, or, in matchplay form, with each player playing against the other two. The more common form of play other than straightforward singles, is in groups of four. There are several ways of playing like this; firstly in 'foursomes,' also labelled by the Americans as 'Scotch foursomes'. In this, each pair only plays one ball between them, hitting alternate shots on each hole, but with one of the partnership always driving on each of the odd holes and the other taking the evens. Again

one can either play this in some form of medal or matchplay. Or again, still in fours, one can play in 'fourballs,' certainly in Britain a more common form of play amongst men than women. In this each player plays one ball, usually taking the better score of the partnership for each hole. So one is not limited in golf to playing in pairs, but can always play in threes and fours – bearing in mind, however, that as beginners a threeball or fourball is very slow and a ladies' fourball is unlikely to be unanimously welcomed on most courses!

As well as being able to play in threes and fours in this way, the forms of competition one can play embrace far more than just the medal play or matchplay rounds. Medal play is generally

considered to be the best test of golf, for every shot counts, whereas in matchplay it doesn't really matter whether one loses a hole with a six or a twelve. Most clubs therefore organize rather more popular forms of competition than the medal play round. These usually take the form of 'flag competitions,' 'Stableford bogeys,' 'bogeys' and several others, often slightly different or with slightly different names from one country to another. These are outlined in the section on golfing terminology but you will usually find your committee member or professional willing to explain the method of playing these competitions as they crop up.

The rules

As far as the rules of golf go they are decidedly complex. After all one isn't playing on a court or ground which is entirely uniform world wide so that new problems arise time and time again which require rulings from the two chief governing bodies of world golf – the Royal and Ancient in St. Andrews and the United States Golf Association – before they can be satisfactorily solved by the existing rules. You will hardly find a member in your club who will know the rules absolutely thoroughly. They are complicated and there is no getting away from this. But in starting to play golf do make sure firstly that you own a rule book and secondly that you read it through every now and then to refresh your memory so that you at least pick up all the basic

major rules and know where to find the rest of them.

Don't merely believe what other people tell you but check this information when you can. It really is surprising how many golfers play under the wrong rules when something rather unusual arises. Most golfers think they know the rules very much more thoroughly than they really do. Certainly they know the basics but the rules that are perhaps only used once or twice a year are often misused, quite unintentionally, and often to the disadvantage of the player. Personally I go through the rule book from cover to cover about three times a year just to make sure I am not misinterpreting anything or failing to make full use of some rule. Financially I can't afford to make

poor use of the rules, for if I used them wrongly I could be disqualified; using them correctly I could save myself several strokes. So try at some stage in your first year as a golfer to look as thoroughly as you can at the rules. On the whole you will find more of them a help than a hindrance so they are well worth knowing.

Well, that's a start to the game. It may sound as if there is a great deal to learn but it will all take shape gradually and, as a rule, golfers are pretty sympathetic to beginners. We all started as beginners once, and because it is such a complex game it teaches us all a lesson from time to time. So be prepared to ask for advice, be prepared to read and take plenty of good, professional instruction.

16 LESSONS EQUIPMENT AND PRACTICE

Getting the most from tuition

Learning and youth

Golf is one of the sports in which good and thorough coaching is most important. Most games and sports which women learn are learnt at school or at school age, when learning is comparatively easy. By contrast, the vast majority of golfers take up the game as adults. This, in itself, makes learning much more difficult and considerably slower. One tends to have set types of actions very strongly patterned from other games; new actions becoming increasingly more difficult to learn with age. Of course, one can become a very fine golfer without starting as a child, but the optimum age for learning is probably between about seven and twelve. At this age new skills are learnt quickly and simply, and even if the enthusiasm for golf is not there, the basic learning developed at this stage is almost always noticeable for the pupil who returns to golf as an adult. For children I think formal teaching should be kept to a few basic lessons, ideally in groups where possible. Children of this age learn by imitation very much more than by words, so that by far the best way of learning is just through watching a really good player. Children are very, very easy to teach.

The woman beginner

But for adults, and women in particular, good golf teaching really is important. Men, as a rule, develop a natural swing – not necessarily a correct one – so that they can usually make some start at the game with very few basic lessons. On the other hand, women often find it very nearly impossible to hit the ball at all without plenty of advice in the beginning. For the complete beginner my advice would be to try to join a class for a series of ten or twenty lessons, followed straight away by some individual ones. Women beginning to play golf tend to be self-conscious; they find the basics difficult and often get discouraged very early on. By learning in a class or even in a group of three or four, one has the advantage of watching everyone else finding the same difficulties. Group lessons also provide a cheaper way of having a longer course of instruction. In private lessons much of the professional's time is understandably taken up in watching the beginner's practice attempts and just repeating the same advice over and over again. In a class lesson you get plenty of advice and yet time to practise on your own with the professional keeping a watchful eye on you from a distance. He will soon come to your rescue if anything goes wrong.

The difficulty of unlearning

Having moved on from the beginner's stage, don't stop having lessons too soon. Go through every part of the game with your professional – putting, chipping and pitching, bunker shots and anything else you find difficult on the course. It is a great mistake to struggle on without plenty of good tuition. Once you start playing a shot incorrectly it can be very, very difficult to unlearn the faulty action – much more difficult than learning the right way in the first place. At this stage try to avoid too much advice from friends and family. They only mean to be helpful but golf isn't an easy game to play even reasonably well. The chances are they don't play the shot correctly themselves and are only likely to pass the fault on to you. Of course, if they have been in the single figure handicap range themselves they may be quite helpful but otherwise let the advice go straight in one ear and out the other!

Learning on the course

For the more advanced player I think the finest way of learning more about the game is to divide your time between lessons on the practice ground and a few teaching lessons on the course. If the professional will take you out on the course for an hour, watching you play five or six holes, it gives him, or her, a chance to see just where you go wrong in scoring as well as being able to help you with some of the finesse shots around the green. This is where one really has to improve to get into the single figure handicap range. Something I would avoid is changing from one professional to another too often. If you go to a new pro always be prepared to go for three or four lessons in quick succession, telling the professional that you intend to do this. He then knows you aren't expecting absolute miracles and he can tackle the flaws in your swing very thoroughly and methodically over a period. If he feels you may only have come for an instant cure he may not like to work on any really radical changes. So put your professional in the picture; tell him whether you are expecting a mid-season pep talk and check up or a complete overhaul! In this way you give him a fair chance to do the very best he can for you.

Choosing a set of clubs

The other way in which you can buy yourself a better game is through having good equipment. It doesn't necessarily have to be brand new. The important thing with a set of clubs is that it is well balanced and suitable for your size and strength. Once more look to your professional for advice. He is trained to assist you in this way and to alter any clubs to your needs.

Clubs for the beginner

As far as a set for the beginner or longer handicap golfer is concerned, it is much better to start with a limited number of clubs, rather than a full set of fourteen. A full set of clubs is probably only an advantage for the silver division golfer and absolutely necessary for the single figure player. It is much better to start with a few clubs, learning to play each of these well, rather than having a full set, none of which you really feel happy with. The one thing I would stress to the beginner is to choose a make of clubs which can be built up over a relatively long period of time. Women, as a rule, don't start with a full set and there is nothing worse than trying to add to a set, only to find the model has gone out of production or changed in design. So ask your professional to put you onto a make and model which you will be able to add to as you need.

Having chosen a good make and model, decide what numbers you need to start your first set. For the absolute beginner a few good clubs to start with are the 2-wood, a 6-iron and sand wedge plus the putter. This will give you the basic minimum – the wood to drive with, the 6-iron for making progress up the fairway and for chipping round the green, a sand wedge for getting up and over trouble and out of bunkers, and the putter. These clubs are easy to carry in a light bag and yet sufficient to give you a start in every part of the game.

Adding to your clubs

From this 'starter's set,' I would add in turn the 8-iron, a 4- or 5-wood and the 4-iron – giving what is called a 'half set'. This half, the even irons, is my own preference. Many pros would rather sell the odd numbered irons, in which case you would probably start with a 5-iron instead of the 6. My own feeling is that while this is fine for men, the 3-iron is a difficult club for most women and the player who is able to use this well is usually ready for a full set. The 5-wood is by far a more useful club. From here you can gradually add the rest of the irons as you feel you find a use for them, with the addition of a driver once the 2-wood becomes really easy to manage and the flight it produces is high and straight. As for a choice of the set of woods for a woman golfer I would suggest a 1, 3, 4 and 5 for the really good player, and either a 1, 3 and 5 or 2, 4 and 5 for the higher handicap; this really depends on how good a grip you have and so whether you can produce sufficient carry with the driver. Once again look to the professional who teaches you for advice.

What to look for in a club

Length and shaft

A standard set of ladies' clubs should suit almost every woman golfer, from say 4 feet 10 inches to 5 feet 9 inches in height, and above 6 or 7 handicap. Because one is short it doesn't necessarily mean one needs a shorter club. If one is short, one usually has fairly short arms and if one is tall one usually has rather longer arms, so that the position of the hands at address doesn't vary as enormously as one might expect. The standard length of clubs is therefore quite suitable for a surprisingly large range of sizes and builds. For the really small player or for anyone taking up golf in her sixties, a junior club may be better, but on the whole it is only the taller and better player who needs any alteration in length. In this case one can move on to a club of men's length – an inch longer per club – but also changing to an A, or number 3, shaft. Incidentally, it is the shaft more than anything which determines the price of different models of clubs. The more expensive shaft has more 'step-downs' – those little rings around the shaft – giving it a slightly more consistent flexing or bending and also often being rather harder wearing. A cheaper shaft is often perfectly serviceable but the 'feel' one gets for the clubhead isn't always quite as good and the club may seem rather lifeless. As a beginner you are very much in the hands of the professional, but as you get more experienced with the game you will soon be able to pick up a club and tell whether it feels right for you.

As far as weight goes this, too, is fairly standard, the better golfer again being able to move onto something slightly more powerful, something between the ordinary men's and ladies' model.

For this calibre of player it is very tempting to move straight to an ordinary men's set, but unless one is very good and plays a great deal this can be a mistake. Women tend to suffer from tiredness on the golf course much more quickly than men, so that although a standard men's set may feel fine on the practice ground, remember it still has to feel right after eighteen or even thirty-six holes. So be very sure before you go for anything too heavy and powerful. In my own set I have woods of regular men's length and weight, but I also have two sets of irons – an A shaft which I use in Britain and an R shaft (the regular men's one) which I often use in hotter conditions and during a tournament season when I am playing every day. If I had to choose between the two, I would select the A shaft. It is better to have a club which is on the light side rather than one which is too heavy and so begins to swing you.

The lie

The one thing you really may find differing from set to set is the lie of the club. This really refers to the way in which the club sits. If you set an iron club to the ball with your hands in a comfortable position, the toe of the club should be just a fraction off the ground; room, say, for a small coin to be slid under it. As you make contact with the ball, the flexing of the shaft brings the sole perfectly flush with the ground. This is important. If the toe is well off the ground, the heel is likely to catch in the turf, pulling or hooking the ball to the left. Here the club is too upright and is more suitable for a player who holds her hands higher at address or for a taller player. This is the fault the smaller player may find with an ordinary set. On the other hand, if the heel is off the ground, the toe is likely to catch in it, producing a slice – this time the club being more suited to the smaller golfer or one with a low hand position. Don't try to alter the position of your hands to suit the club; the professional can easily change the lies to suit you.

So in choosing clubs look to your professional, not just for help in selecting a good model but for any after sale adjustments you may need. This is where he can score over the sports shop or department store.

Other equipment

Shoes

As well as golf clubs there are several other fairly necessary items of golfing equipment. Firstly golf shoes. In winter it really is essential to wear a pair of spiked shoes; without them it is virtually impossible to get a firm grip with the feet to create speed in the swing without losing balance. My own preference is for a leather upper to the shoe, but with a rubber sole. The rubber sole gives the flexibility needed while the leather upper is tough with plenty of support. A leather sole, by contrast, never seems flexible enough; my foot bends but the shoe doesn't bend with it – leaving me with blisters on the back of my heel. This is my own experience with golf shoes, but it is a tip which may help you find a really comfortable pair. When you consider that you have to walk up to five miles in a round of golf it makes sense to be comfortable. In the summer by all means wear a light pair of shoes without spikes, but make sure that you really can grip well without them. Good footwear is essential to good golf.

Gloves

Secondly, gloves. A golf glove is by no means a necessity, but for the newer player or for anyone who plays or practises a great deal it should avoid blisters. Added to this it gives a more consistent grip, whether one's hands are warm or cold or a little moist. The generally accepted thing is to wear the left hand glove alone. This is the hand which is completely on the club so that the glove helps in making this grip firmer and less likely to slip. The glove should be tight when you put it on – very much tighter than an ordinary glove. When it is put on for the first time it should feel just about as tight as possible, providing none of the seams are obviously strained. A really good golf glove is made of very thin leather so treat it gently and ease your fingers down into it one at a time. After the first couple of minutes with the glove on, it should mould well to your hand just like an extra layer of skin, giving you a firm grip on the club but without any loss of feeling through it. In the winter try to avoid wearing two gloves. The addition of the right hand one often changes the whole character of the grip and with it the pattern of shots. So instead, if the weather is cold, a better idea is to carry a thick pair of sheepskin mittens, putting them on between shots and just wearing the left hand glove as usual.

A golf ball to suit your game

Lastly, let's look at golf balls. Prices of these range enormously. But the most expensive ball isn't necessarily the best for every standard of golfer. There are three main types of ball to look at. Firstly, there is the ordinary golf ball which is formed of a core of wound rubber, covered with a synthetic casing. The different prices for this type of golf ball vary according to compression. In Britain, at any rate, the hardest compression is marketed as the top grade ball with the slightly softer ball usually being sold as a second grade ball. In manufacture they are really identical and testing of the finished product determines the price they sell at. When we talk of compression what we mean is the ease with which the ball compresses or squashes up as the clubhead strikes it. The harder compression golf ball is more suitable for the really good golfer who has the clubhead speed to be able to compress this standard of ball. The woman golfer, by contrast, is generally unable to make use of the extra hardness of the top grade ball and is much better off, unless she is in the single figure handicap bracket, with the second grade ball from a good manufacturer. In the winter, too, the ball becomes more difficult to compress as the rubber is less active, so once again the extra expense of the better one is really a

waste and often something of a handicap.

The second type of ball is the solid ball – made in one piece from a composition material. This is the type usually used at driving ranges. The enormous advantage of this for the longer handicap golfer is that it is very much stronger and tougher than the conventional ball. Where the cover of the other ball will cut or split if one doesn't strike it well, the solid ball goes on shot after shot, unmarked but just looking more and more dingy. The disadvantage of this type of ball is that it loses a little distance and perhaps doesn't give the nice 'click' of the wound ball. But, and this is very important, the distance lost with this type of ball is really only very slight for the longer handicap golfer or beginner. The scratch golfer will usually lose a few yards on the drive so you are unlikely to see top class amateurs or professionals using a solid ball. However, for the club golfer the extra durability of this ball makes it really ideal.

Lastly, there is the recovered ball – a very cheap way of buying golf balls for the beginner. Here the cores of old, cut golf balls are taken out and recovered to give them a new lease of life. They won't fly quite as well as the original but it is a good way of buying golf balls when you first start and are likely to both cut and lose plenty.

Making the most of your practice

One of the main things about practice is to know just how long and hard to work. For most standards of golfers it is much better to spread out practice sessions so that if possible one can put in half an hour a day, rather than having one four-hour session in a week. With short, regular practice sessions one can tackle the problem afresh each time, where with hours of practice one is likely to develop faults purely through tiredness. So as far as possible, practise little and often.

An aim to your practice

In any practice session have a really specific idea of what you want to improve. If you are working on something definite in the swing then the medium irons are the ones to work with most. Short irons will always flatter the swing, not showing up any faults, while continual practice with the long clubs tends to destroy timing. Once things are going satisfactorily either work through the clubs up to the woods and driver, or move from one club to another as you might on the course. It is always very important to have a real target for each shot and also to be reasonably competitive in some way when you practise. If one just practises without a target or specific aim it is awfully easy to imagine it is all going much better than it really is. Try on the practice ground to simulate the conditions on the course; imagining playing a round on any course you like is a good way of doing this. Hit the drive and then whatever shot you would need for your second, repeating the kind of clubbing you would need for every hole. In this way it makes every shot

mean something and also stops one from just hitting the balls one after another with very little thought. Another way of practising with a purpose is to give yourself a target, between two trees for example, 10 or 15 yards apart, seeing how many consecutive shots you can land within this area. Again it makes you try on every shot and this is important. It makes practice as close as possible to actually playing on the course.

Practise your whole game

Try, too, to practise every part of golf. Don't purely concentrate on driving or the long game but do plenty of work on chipping, pitching and bunker shots – the part I find most golfers ignore. Putting is something one can always work on on the carpet at home. Even if it is only practising to a matchbox or into an upturned glass it will help groove a consistent stroke. Improvement in the short game may not seem as satisfying to the beginner as developing the long game but this is the part which often makes so much difference to actually scoring. It takes a great deal of work on the long game to take off a stroke a hole, but the beginner can often improve the scores this amount just by working on chipping and putting.

Know when to practise

Lastly, know when to practise. Don't just work at grooving your faults. If things aren't going well try to have a lesson and put them right as soon as possible. If you try to work it out for yourself without having a reasonable amount of knowledge about the swing you are only likely to work yourself into something even worse, from there having to put in a lot of time on unlearning these bad habits. The time to practise most is when things are going really well. This is the time when you can really groove a good swing and make it consistent and repetitive. Practice really is a vital part of the game for the golfer of every standard. Every good golfer practises. Some may practise more than others but success doesn't just happen without a certain degree of hard work. It is true there are golfers who say they have never had a lesson and never practised. They may play reasonably well, but one always wonders just how good they could have been with the addition of both good professional advice and some hard work. So practise little and often; practise most when things are going smoothly and take time to work on every part of the game.

A final piece of advice

Golf is a difficult and sometimes frustrating game to learn. Much of the difficulty for the club golfer is in sorting out and believing just how simple the swing can be, while realizing just how much is involved in

actually scoring well round the golf course.

To my mind the game of golf has two very distinct parts – the actual swing and the ability to score well. I think if the golfer can look upon the swing as

being comparatively simple – bearing in mind that a child can usually master it quite quickly – but think of the reason why it is often hard to score well and hit the ball correctly under the pressure of competition, then I think he or she will do very much better. In the actual swing I would always look first to the grip for the source of trouble, from there to the lining up of the shoulders, watching the ball and continuing the swing right through to a balanced follow-through. With all these in check one is likely to avoid the totally disastrous shots of golf. And this is very much what the game is about – making one's bad shots fewer and less destructive. Golf is very much a game of mistakes and is one in which ability varies from day to day perhaps more than any other. One day you think you have all the answers; the next they let you down completely. You always go out not quite knowing what that round has in store for you, and that, perhaps, is the true fascination of golf. One never does stop learning. But whatever you want from your golf – whether you want to be a champion or just an average club golfer – I hope you get as much enjoyment from learning golf as I get from both playing and teaching it. It is an exacting game and for some a very difficult game, but it is also a very great game. I hope that in some way this book and these lessons on golf will help you both improve and enjoy the game to its fullest.

GLOSSARY

Address – the stationary position in which one prepares to hit the ball.

Airshot – the height of embarrassment for the beginner – missing the ball completely.

Albatross – an unusual term for an unusual golfing feat, a hole completed in three less than the par (or standard) score. In America more commonly known as a 'double eagle,' an eagle being two under par.

All Square – in matchplay where the players are even in the match.

Backspin – it is the fact that the ball takes up backspin which keeps it flying through the air. A skilled player can also put on extra backspin, meaning that the ball lands on the green and stops almost on this spot.

Backswing – the first half of the swing in which the club is swung up away from the ball to around the right shoulder.

Better Ball – this refers to a kind of partnership scoring in which the better score by either of the partnership is recorded for each hole.

Birdie – a hole completed in one under the par (standard) score.

Bisque – in a match or bogey competition a stroke which can be taken where one chooses instead of at an allotted hole. This is taken after completion of the hole.

Blaster – an alternative name for the most lofted club in the set, more commonly known as the sand wedge or sand iron.

Bogey – in Britain an alternative name for par though rather dying out now and taking on the American meaning for a hole completed in one over par.

Bogey Competition – this is a competition in which the player plays a hole by hole match against par (bogey). The player receives ¾ of the handicap and takes these in the form of strokes from par according to the stroke index. Unlike in a true match the whole round is completed and the player records how many up or down she is against par, e.g., 3 up, 6 down. This is generally a most difficult form of competition.

Borrow – in putting, if the surface of the green is not horizontal one has to aim to the right or left to allow for this slope. In this case one says one 'borrows to the right' or 'borrows to the left.'

Brassie – this is another name for the 2-wood. Whereas the 1-wood is almost always known as the driver, 'brassie' is a relatively uncommon name for the 2-wood.

Bronze Division – in ladies' golf, players are termed as being in the bronze division or silver division according to handicap. The bronze division includes all players with handicaps from 19 to 36 while the silver division is the better players with handicaps below 18.

Bunker – this is a depression in the ground designed to catch a ball hit offline. As a rule the term 'bunker' implies that this is full of sand, but it can also refer to a 'grass bunker.'

Bye – in matchplay the match is often won by one side before the eighteenth hole. In this case the remaining holes can be played as a separate, unofficial match known as the 'bye.'

Caddie – a person employed by a player or partnership of players to carry the bag and give advice on anything concerned with the course or the game.

Casual Water – whenever water lies on the course, which is clearly not designed to be there in the form of a ditch or pond, this is known as 'casual water.' One can drop away from this without penalty, either if the ball is in the water or if one is forced to stand in the water. If your ball is on the green and there is water between you and the hole you may move to the closest place, equal distance from the hole, where you can avoid putting through this.

Centre-Shaft – with conventional clubs, the shaft is joined to the head of the club at one end of the club, known as the 'heel.' However, in certain putters the shaft is joined very much more towards the middle of the head – these being referred to as 'centre-shafted' putters.

Chip – a short running shot from just off the edge of the green, using one of the medium irons.

Cleats – an American alternative for the spikes in golf shoes which help give the player better grip and balance.

Closed – this is a technical term concerning the relationship between the direction of the stance and clubface. The clubface is 'closed' if it faces off to the left of the direction in which you hope to hit the ball. The stance is 'closed' if the feet aim off to the right of target. In both cases the stance and clubface 'close' or converge to the target.

Cup – an alternative term for the hole when referring to the actual hole cut in the green. The true meaning is the metal lining which is sunk in the hole.

Dead – in matchplay if one's opponent's ball is so close to the hole that one can safely assume she will put it in, about a foot or less, then one describes the ball as being 'dead' and can concede or 'give' her the putt. In stroke play one can refer to a ball a few inches from the hole as being dead but one still has to tap it into the hole – and one *can* miss from very short range!

Divot – in playing an iron shot correctly the ball should be struck, followed by the clubhead passing on down and through the turf, cutting out a sliver of turf a few inches long, known as a 'divot.'

Dormie – supposing in matchplay I finish the fifteenth hole 3 up against my opponent. I am now in the happy position of knowing that with only three holes left to play, if she should win all of these she can still only pull up level with me by the completion of the round. I am then said to be 'dormie 3 up' and she is 'dormie 3 down.' In a knock-out tournament this has less meaning than in team matches. If in a tournament one completes the round all-square then extra holes are played until one player is ahead. So the player who is dormie 3 up could still lose by playing extra holes. However, in team matches one usually only plays to the eighteenth so that a halved match may be recorded. In this case the player who is dormie 3 up is certain not to lose.

Downswing – the part of the swing from the top of the backswing down to the impact of the ball.

Draw – a controlled shot which curves very slightly from right to left in the air.

Driver – this is the common name for the most powerful club in the set, the 1-wood. This is the club designed for getting maximum length from the tee – the shot from the tee with the driver or 2-wood being a 'drive.'

Eagle – a hole completed in two less than the par (standard) score.

Eclectic – a type of competition run over a period of weeks or months as a rule, in which the player records her best score for every hole taken over the period. After completing the initial round, in other words, she is trying to improve the scores for each individual hole.

Explosion Shot – a shot from a bunker where the ball is buried or partly buried and it is splashed out with plenty of sand.

Face – the face of the club is the part of the clubhead from which the ball is struck.

Face Insert – a hard wearing piece of material, usually plastic, inset into the face of wooden clubs.

Fade – the opposite of a draw – a shot which bends slightly from left to right in the air.

Fairway – the cut part of the course between the tee and green along which one is supposed to play.

Fairway Woods – these are the 2-, 3-, 4- and 5-woods and, unlike the driver (1-wood) are designed to be hit not just from the tee but also from the fairway. Of these the 2-wood is the most difficult so that many players only use this as an alternative to the driver.

Flag – this marks the position of the hole so that one sees it from a distance.

Flag Competition – in this competition the player is allotted a certain number of strokes to use for the round – the par of the course plus her handicap. In other words a 30 handicap golfer playing on a par 70 course is given 100 strokes to use. After using all these strokes she places a flag with her name on where her hundredth shot finishes and the person who finishes nearest the eighteenth hole or furthest on up the first or second fairway is the winner.

Flange – this is the name for the broad sole of an iron club, particularly of the sand wedge where the flange can be very wide and bulbous.

Flat Swing – a swing where the club travels very low round the body in both backswing and throughswing.

Followthrough – this is the part of the swing beyond the impact with the ball, for a full drive the club going right on over the left shoulder and down the back.

Fore – this is the word to shout if you think there is a chance of your ball hitting anyone. If you hear a shout of 'Fore' don't look round to see whether they mean you, instead put your arms over your head, stoop over and hope that if it is coming your way it at least misses hitting you on the head. A golf ball can kill, so take note of this.

Fourball – a form of play where four players play together, using a ball each, but generally in partnerships. The form here is often a better ball, taking the better score for the partnership for each hole.

Foursome – in this, four players play together in pairs, but playing one ball between a pair and taking alternate shots for each hole. One player elects to drive every odd hole and the other the evens. The Americans refer to this very often as 'Scotch foursomes.'

Fringe – this is the name for the collar of slightly longer grass just surrounding the putting green.

Grain – some types of grass used on putting greens rather than growing uniformly upright tend to lie in a certain direction, either because of the nearness of water or mountains or with the rising and setting of the sun. This then has to be taken into account as well as assessing the slope of the green, for the ball tends to run with the grain of the grass.

Green – the green or putting green is the manicured area in which the hole is cut.

Greensome – this is a form of play in which players go out in fours, made up of two pairs. All four players drive on each hole. The players of each partnership choose the better drive of their two and finish the hole playing alternate shots, the player whose drive was not taken playing the second shot. The handicap of the pair is taken as $^6/_{10}$ of the lower handicap plus $^4/_{10}$ of the higher handicap.

Grip – this refers to the way in which the club is held and to the leather binding or rubber sleeve which covers the end of the shaft.

Ground Under Repair – areas on the course which are in the process of repair or alteration may be designated by the committee as 'ground under repair.' One can pick and drop the ball without penalty so that one neither has to hit the ball from ground under repair, nor stand in ground under repair nor putt through ground under repair on the green. If a ball is definitely lost in ground under repair another ball is dropped just outside it without penalty.

Gross Score – this is the actual score in which one completes the course, before any deduction of handicap.

Half, Halved – a hole is said to be a 'half' or 'halved' if the opponents register the same score, or the same score after deduction of handicap. A match is halved if players complete the eighteenth hole all square.

Handicap – this is measure of a player's general standard relative to par for the course. Thus on a par 70 course, a 30 handicap golfer is expected to go round in 100 if playing to her best, or near to her best standard.

Hanging Lie – this refers to a difficult position in golf, when one plays off ground sloping downhill in the direction in which you are hitting.

Hazard – this includes sand bunkers, and ditches, ponds or lakes which are termed as 'water hazards.' In these one cannot ground the club in addressing the ball nor remove any loose impediments (see later).

Heel – although the part of the club which hits the ball is known as the clubhead, the parts of it sound more like a foot – the heel being the end where the shaft joins the head, with the toe at the other end and the sole underneath.

Hole – this refers to the hole cut in the green and to each of the eighteen playing areas from tee to green. So if, for example, one refers to the 'ninth hole' one usually means the whole area embracing the ninth tee to the ninth green and all the rough, fairway and hazards in between.

Hole-in-one – the ambition of all golfers – hitting the tee shot straight into the hole.

Honour – the winner of every hole then assumes 'the honour' on the next tee, meaning that she drives first. If holes are halved the player holds on to the honour until her opponent wins a hole. She then takes the honour and drives first.

Hooded – the clubface is said to be 'hooded' when it is turned in slightly, reducing its effective loft.

Hook – a shot which bends very severely from right to left in the air.

Hosel – the shaft and iron head are manufactured separately. The part of the clubhead which extends upwards and into which the shaft is fitted is known as the 'hosel.'

Lateral Water Hazard – ditches or ponds which run roughly parallel to the line of the hole are termed 'lateral water hazards.' Whereas with an ordinary water hazard one would pick out behind the hazard for a penalty stroke, with a lateral hazard one still takes the same penalty but can drop the ball to either side of it.

Lie – firstly this refers to the way in which the ball sits on the ground. If the grass is lush and the ball sits up well, we say it is a good lie; if the ground is bare or the ball sits in a slight depression we say the lie is bad or 'tight.' Secondly, this refers to the angle between the clubhead and the shaft which makes a set of clubs more suitable for a tall or short golfer. A club with an upright lie is more suitable to a taller golfer and a club with a flat lie for the shorter golfer.

Local Rules – where there are unusual features or unusual conditions on a course which are not covered by the rules of golf, the club committee can make additional rules to clarify such points, these being termed 'local rules' and usually being listed on the back of the scorecard.

Loft – to give a full range of shots through the set of clubs, the angle of the clubface is graded from around 12° with the driver to 57° with the sand wedge. This is termed the 'loft' of the club, with the sand wedge being the most 'lofted' club.

Loose Impediments – these are natural objects such as twigs or leaves which may be moved from around the ball, providing firstly that they are not growing and secondly that they are not actually adhering to the ball. Care must, however, be taken in moving these for if the ball moves this is a penalty of an extra stroke. Although this applies 'through the green,' one may not move loose impediments in a hazard.

Lost Ball – if a ball is lost, except in a water hazard or casual water or ground under repair (all of which are covered by specific rules) one returns to the spot from where the ball was hit and drops another ball, or from the tee re-tees another ball. One is then playing two more than the stroke with which the original ball was lost, e.g., if one's third shot was lost, one would return to the spot where it was hit from, drop another ball and hit stroke five. One is only allowed to search for a ball for five minutes and then it must be assumed to be lost.

Mark, Marker – on the green one may lift the ball and 'mark' its position either to clean it or if one's opponent or partner indicates that it is in her way. The procedure for this is to place a small round 'marker,' such as a coin, behind the ball before lifting it. The ball is then replaced in the same spot ahead of the marker before the marker is lifted. The player who marks your card in a competition is also correctly known as the 'marker.'

Matchplay – this is the form of competition in which one competes hole by hole against one individual or a partnership, rather than competing against the whole field of players as in 'stroke play.' On each hole the player with the lower score wins the hole and records her score as 1 up, 2 up and so on, while the opponent would be 1 down, 2 down etc. One player wins when she is sufficient holes up that the opponent could not catch her even if she won all the remaining ones – for example, if she were five up with only four holes to play, in which case she is said to win by '5 & 4.'

Medal – a medal round is another name for stroke play where it is the total score for the course which is recorded, rather than hole by hole scoring against another player.

Nett Score – in a handicap competition the player's total score for the course is recorded as the gross score. The handicap is deducted and this new total is the 'nett score.' Thus a 30 handicap golfer completing the course in a gross score of 98 would have a nett score of 68.

Nineteenth – if a match is all square after eighteen holes, play continues on down the first, second and so on until one player wins a hole. The first then becomes the nineteenth, the second the twentieth and so on. The nineteenth is also a popular name for the club bar.

Nose – colloquial name for the toe of the club.

Obstruction – this is anything unnatural built or left on the course, other than roads or fences which form the boundary of the course. These fall into two groups, movable and immovable – if it isn't obvious whether the object is movable or not this will often be defined in local rules, for example a heavy seat. If an obstruction is movable, one simply goes ahead and moves it; if the obstruction is immovable then the ball can be dropped away from it so that it does not interfere with the swing.

Open – just the opposite, as one might expect, of closed. If the clubface faces off to the right of the target it is said to be open; if the feet aim off to the left of the target the stance is open. In other words the lines of clubface and stance diverge or open to the target.

Out of Bounds – this is ground – usually outside the boundary of the course – on which play is prohibited. If a fence marks out of bounds then it is the inside of the fence which is taken as the out of bounds line. However, the ball is only out of bounds if the whole of it is outside this line. If a ball goes out of bounds one has to hit another shot from the spot where the original was played from, now playing two shots more than the original one.

Outside Agency – this is a name given to someone or something outside the match or competition who may have an influence on the ball. Thus if the ball is deflected while it is moving by a spectator or animal – the outside agency – this is said to be a 'rub of the green;' in other words luck or bad luck and the ball has to be played from where it finishes. Once the ball comes to rest any action of an outside agency is of no consequence, for the ball is simply replaced where it was without penalty.

Par – this is the figure for every hole in which the really top class player would be expected to complete it. A par-3 hole would require one shot onto the green, plus an allowance of two putts, the par-4 hole would require two shots plus the two putt allowance and the par-5 three shots to the green plus two putts. The total of the eighteen pars would then give the par of the course.

Peg – a plastic or wooden peg (or tee-peg) may be used on the teeing ground to raise the ball slightly off the ground in order to help produce the very best possible shot.

Penalty – in stroke play the penalty for playing a rule incorrectly is generally the addition of two strokes and in matchplay almost always loss of the hole.

Pin – another name for the flag.

Pitch Mark – any ball landing on a soft green from much height or distance usually cuts up a little turf as it lands – a pitch mark. Every player should repair the marks she makes in this way but one is always allowed to repair these marks if they interfere with the line of the putt.

Pitch Shot – a high, lofted shot to the green, usually played with the 9-iron, 10-iron or sand wedge and in distance, ranging from 25 or 30 yards to a full shot with these clubs.

Plus Handicap – a plus handicap golfer is almost always one of international standard and is rated as being better than scratch, where a scratch golfer is one who is expected to play virtually faultless golf and so complete the course in par figures. Thus on a course with a standard scratch of 72 a plus 1 golfer is expected to go round in 71, the plus 2 golfer in 70 and so on. Players below plus 2 are something of a rarity.

Provisional Ball – if it seems possible that a ball is lost (except in a water hazard) or out of bounds, then to save time a provisional ball may be played from this spot and played up to where the lost ball is likely to be. If the original ball is lost or out of bounds then the provisional ball becomes the one in play but for two strokes more than the shot with which the original ball was lost. If the original ball is found in bounds the provisional ball cannot be used.

Pull – this is the shot which flies straight left of target.

Push – this is the opposite of the pull and is a shot which flies straight right of target.

Putt, Putter and Putting Green – the putting green is the area in which the hole is cut. The type of shot used on the green is the putt with the club used being the putter.

Rough – this is the area of long or uncut grass bordering the fairway. Although this is entirely different from the fairway and can be very difficult to play from, the rules of golf do not actually distinguish between the two.

Royal and Ancient – the Royal and Ancient Golf Club of St. Andrews – the R. & A. – is the governing body of golf in Great Britain and along with the United States Golf Association revises and administers the rules of golf worldwide.

Rub of the Green – when a ball is stopped or deflected, while it is moving, by an outside agency, i.e., someone or something outside the game – this is known as a 'rub of the green' and the ball has to be played as it lies, whether it is an advantage or disadvantage to the player.

Rules – the rules of golf as laid down by the R. & A. and U.S.G.A. are the same throughout the world, except for the local rules laid down by clubs, or in some cases associations, to deal with specific situations not covered by the rules of golf.

Sand Trap – an alternative name for a bunker.

Sand Wedge, Sand Iron – the most lofted club in the set, especially designed for getting out of bunkers.

Scratch Player – the scratch golfer is the measure from which the par and standard scratch of the course are assessed. The scratch golfer is therefore expected to complete the course in par, meaning that, as a rule, she is of international class.

Set of Clubs – the maximum number of clubs one can use in a set is fourteen. As a rule this is made up of four woods, nine irons and a putter or three woods, ten irons and a putter.

Shaft – the shaft of the club is usually made of steel but can also be made of wood (hickory), aluminium, carbon fibre or fibre glass. It is the quality of the shaft which usually determines the overall quality of the club. These vary in flexibility to suit different standards of player, either graded numerically upwards as the shaft becomes whippier, or L denoting a ladies' shaft, A a light men's shaft, R a regular shaft and S a stiff shaft.

Shank – this is the name given both to the part of the iron club where the face joins the hosel and in turn the shaft, and also to a shot where the ball is hit from this part of the club. Because of the angle of this part of the club the shot it produces flies off to the right most markedly. For this reason it is one of the most disastrous shots in golf and one of the most difficult to cure.

Shot – see under 'stroke.'

Shut – an alternative to 'closed.'

Silver Division – this division in ladies' golf includes all handicaps from plus to 18.

Single – a match in which one player plays against another.

Skied Shot – this is a shot which takes off with tremendous, unintentional height, usually with a driver, where the ball is struck with the top of the club instead of the clubface.

Slice – this is a shot which bends severely from left to right in the air.

Socket – another name for the 'shank' – both the part of the club and the shot produced from this.

Sole – this is the bottom of the clubhead, so the part resting on the ground. With a wooden club this generally takes the form of a metal sole-plate, usually aluminium in the driver and 2-wood, and brass in the 3, 4 and 5.

Spikes – also 'studs' or 'cleats' which give the sole of golf shoes the necessary grip for good footwork.

Spoon – another name for the 3-wood and in some cases also applied to the 4. Like the term 'brassie' for the 2-wood this is by no means as commonly used as 'driver' is for the 1-wood.

Square – this is the ideal position for hitting the ball straight, in which the clubface is aimed on target, with the line of the stance parallel to this. Also an alternative for 'all square' where a match is even.

Stableford or **Stableford Bogey** – a form of competition against par (derived from the old name for par of 'bogey'). In this the player takes 7/8 handicap against par according to the stroke index, counting 2 points for a hole completed in par, or nett par, 1 point for a score or nett score of one over par, 3 points for a birdie or nett birdie, 4 for an eagle and so on. The player with the most points for the eighteen holes wins – with winning scores usually ranging from around 35 to 42 points.

Standard Scratch Score – this is the assessment from which all handicaps are taken. The standard scratch score, or par, is the measure of an almost faultless round of golf and is usually only bettered by professionals or top class amateurs.

Stroke – as well as being the name for any shot in golf, this also refers to a handicap stroke received by a player on any hole. Thus a poorer player receives a specific number of strokes or shots from a good player, on the holes where she receives a stroke deducting one from her actual score for the hole before matching it with her opponent.

Stroke and Distance – when a ball is lost or out of bounds or in some cases if it is declared unplayable, one has to return to the spot where the ball was played from, dropping another ball and taking a penalty of 'stroke and distance.' One is then playing two more than the original shot. Thus if the third shot on a hole were lost, one would return to the spot it was hit from, now playing stroke number five.

Stroke Index – this is provided on the card and indicates the holes on which handicap strokes are received. Thus a player in receipt of 10 strokes from her opponent or in a bogey competition takes these on all the holes with the figure 10 or less beside them in the stroke index column.

Stroke Play – the most testing form of competition in which the total number of strokes taken for the whole eighteen holes is recorded. One is therefore playing, not against one specific opponent, but against a whole field of players. For this reason the rules and penalties for matchplay and stroke play are somewhat different.

Strong Grip – a grip in which the left hand is very much on top of the club with the right very much beneath it is known as a 'strong grip.' Although this implies that it is a good grip, it is not. It tends both to reduce the height and carry of shots and also produc-es a severe hook to the ball. For this reason it is alternatively known as the 'hooker's grip.'

Studs – alternative to 'spikes.'

Swingweight – this is a measure of balance and overall weight of golf clubs, used for matching clubs to one another. Ladies' clubs range from around C4 to C9 as they become heavier, with men's clubs going from around D0 to about D7.

Tee or **Teeing Ground** – this is the whole area for teeing off. Very often each hole may have four separate teeing grounds, the ladies' tee, the men's tee and often a forward men's tee and a competition tee. Also 'tee' refers to the peg the ball is put on to raise it off the ground for the tee shot.

Tee Box or **Tee Marker** – this indicates the area of the teeing ground to be used and is moved from day to day to preserve the condition of the teeing ground or to vary the exact length of the hole. One may not tee up ahead of the tee marker but can go back up to two clublengths. In some cases there is just one tee box, in other cases there are two, one each side of the tee, to give a definite guide to the area being used. In each case the tee boxes are distinctly marked to show which is the ladies' tee and which is the men's, but they are not uniformly marked from one course to another.

Three off the Tee – if the ball is lost or out of bounds from the tee, then one has to return to the tee, add a penalty stroke and so play 'three off the tee.' In some cases one may have to do this if the ball is badly unplayable.

Throughswing – the swing through the ball to the follow-through.

Through the Green – this is the whole area of the course except any hazards and the tee and green of the hole being played. There is no distinction in the rules between the rough and fairway.

Tiger Tee – this is another name for the men's back or tournament tee.

Toe – the toe of the club is the part of the clubhead furthest from the shaft, the other end being the heel.

Topped Shot – this is a shot where the clubhead strikes the ball right on or near its top and so sends it straight along the ground with little or no loft.

Trap – an alternative to 'bunker,' more commonly used in America.

Unplayable – a player may deem a ball unplayable anywhere on the course except in a water hazard. With the addition of a penalty stroke the ball can be dropped two clublengths away, not nearer the hole, or as far back as one chooses keeping the spot where the ball lay on line with the hole, or where the original shot was played from. A ball unplayable in a bunker must always be dropped in the bunker.

Upright Swing – a swing in which the club is lifted high above the head in both backswing and throughswing.

Water Hazards – ponds and ditches on the course. One can play from these but the club must not touch the ground at address and one cannot remove any loose impediments. In picking out of a water hazard one adds a penalty stroke, dropping the ball as far back as one likes in line with the spot where it went in. From a lateral hazard, which is one running along the side of the hole, one still takes the penalty stroke but can elect to drop the ball on either side of the hazard within two clublengths of the spot where it entered the hazard.

Weak Grip – this is a grip in which the 'V' between thumb and index finger of either or both hands points to the chin or left of it. The right hand is now very much on top of the club with only one or perhaps two knuckles of the left showing. This results in shots which slice away to the right, and so is also known as the 'slicer's grip.'

Wedge – these are the most lofted irons in the set, the pitching wedge or 10-iron and the sand wedge which is the equivalent of the 11-iron.

Whipping – this is the cord binding around the neck of the head of wooden clubs, in some cases covered with a plastic sleeve.

Wristcock – this is the natural hinging of the wrists which takes place in both backswing and throughswing.